MW01627165

"An amazingly powerful and unforgettable literary debut."

— Sapphire, Author of *Push*

"In a voice as textured as a little girl's cotton summer dress, Regina Louise enthralls you. This well-crafted memoir of longing reminds you of what it means to have a place of your own-especially-a place inside yourself."

— Michael Datcher,
Author of New York Times Bestseller *Raising Fences*

"This is a harsh, often brutal, but always compelling memoir, and its very existence is proof of the author's personal triumph in the face of enormous odds."

— Booklist

"The rare look into the inner world of an unwanted child will enlighten readers concerned with the fate of at-risk children."

- - Publishers Weekly

Someone Has Led This Child To Believe:

A Case History of Love, Luck & Self-Determination

Regina Louise

r&R Press
San Francisco

r&R Books
P.O. Box 2070 #4849
Walnut Creek, CA. 94596
www.thereginalouisefoundation.org
Ordering Information:

Quantity sales. Special discounts are available on quantity purchases by corporations, associations, and others. For details, contact the publisher at the address above.

Orders by U.S. trade bookstores and wholesalers.
Please contact r&R Books:
Tel: 925.222.5896; or visit www.thereginalouisefoundation.org
First r&R Edition,
September 2016
Printed in the United States of America
ISBN 978-0-692-78243-9

Louise, Regina.
Someone has led this child to believe/ Regina Louise

1. Regina Louise.
2. Louise, Regina—Childhood and youth
3. Foster care—United States—Biography—California
4. Black—Poverty—Abandonment—Trauma—Texas
5. California—Recovery

Author can be reached at regina@thereginalouisefoundation.org
Twitter: reginalouises
Facebook: reginalouise
Email: regina@www.thereginalouisefoundation.org

Book design by Sylvie-Marie Dresher

Also By Regina Louise:

Somebody's Someone

This book is dedicated to you who work in the best interest of those who have no say in what it means to be unseen, unheard, and unloved. Thank you for the time you take, the justice you restore, and the possibilities you create. Know that your giving, your compassion and your efforts are not in vain.

Love is Never Wasted

Someone Has Led This Child To Believe

Dear Reader:

The first paid speaking engagement I accepted was offered to me on a crisp, warm day while I sat at my writing desk working on the outline for this book, (which took twelve years to complete by the way.) It was in the fall of 2004, and I resided in Walnut Creek, California by then. I'd recently separated from a ten-year relationship with someone I'd hoped to spend the rest of my life with, but as fate would have it; that aspiration withered on the vine, along with my desire to continue working as a hairstylist and business owner.

I was ready to jump empty-handed into the void. To commit myself to discovering my life's new purpose. This journey led me to complete two higher-education degrees, and establish a foundation dedicated to healing trauma through the Narrative Arts. Most importantly, I discovered that place to which I'd dedicate my life to.

I'd already spoken at various convening's—as conferences are sometimes referenced in the world of Human Services—where the professional teams of social service workers, and executives and lawyers and the like, gathered together to focus on official matters concerning the fate of at-risk children, and the youth within their care.

I marveled at the fact that there were so many people involved in fighting the good fight to improve living circumstances for foster children. These children, our children, were already living with the stigmas of being separated from their families, as well as the consequences from the lingering affects of compounded traumas, ambiguous losses and the resultant costs of disenfranchised grief. So when I was asked to consider that particular speaking request I became critically concerned by what the caller said:

"Hello," I answered. "Are you Regina Louise?" The caller asked. "Yes. I am," I said. "Hi, Regina… I'm in charge of the committee that chooses speakers and your name was mentioned." I was honored to know this, and most excited to consider a chance to contribute to the national narrative regarding the fate of at-risk children and youth.

"Would you be interested in coming to speak to our group about what you know about those 'throw-away kids'?" Thinking the caller was trying out a really bad joke I hesitated to respond. "I'm not sure I understand," I replied, needing time to compose myself. "Which 'throw-away' kids are you referring to?" I asked. I could only assume the caller detected my disturbance. "Oh," she said. "I meant to say… you know… foster kids."

That phone call was brilliant. I choose this word 'brilliant' with the utmost intention. I choose this word because it became the helm from which I would base my commitment to do the work I now do. It became the opening I needed to better understand the nomenclature used—by some—in an effort perhaps, to try and wrap their heads around the staggering numbers of children in out-of-home placements, and their fates once they aged-out.

I believed the caller was making an effort to name the magnitude of the situation, albeit in a not so tactful manner. Nevertheless, it was an opportunity to educate, an opportunity to help others reimagine how we label human beings and the resultant impact that is left with such practices.

Throughout my journey, I have met thousands of children and youth who reside in various forms of out-of-home placements. From group homes to fictive kin homes, from Transitional Housing programs to emancipated young people doing what they can to get through the day. One day at a time. Some seemed to thrive more than others, while there have been many who've felt they can't even "afford to dream beyond an inch of my breath.

So, it is for these individuals, these humans, and the ones who work around the clocks of their hearts to ensure the normalization of the playing field, to close the gap of disadvantage which places the average foster youth at twice the risk of not being able to live their lives in a dignified manner. Limiting. Their. Choices. It is for them that I dare reach back into some dark places in my life, and stare my traumas in the face. Forgive the ones that are forgivable, and learn to live with the ones that are more elusive, less amicable to negotiation, or resistant to meaning making.

I accepted that speaking engagement so many years ago. I am happy that I did. That opportunity allowed me to walk upon a stage, take the podium before hundreds and proudly stand as a possibility of a 'throw-away' child's potential as a result of a person here or there showing me my worth, a person here or there mirroring back to me the vastness of my possibilities. And not so unlike the parable of the feeding of the multitudes, a person here or there modeled the Law of Multiplication for me:

1. *I learned the value of a smile and how to pass happiness on to someone else*
2. *I learned the value of meting out kindness in the return of more kindness*
3. *I learned that the gift of hope is hope*
4. *I learned that generosity carves out a space within for more generosity*
5. *I learned to recognize that I was never truly alone, and that throughout my life there were always another set of footprints. Sometimes they belonged to others, and at other times they were my own.*
6. *I learned, in time, to understand the reciprocal nature of the human spirit*
7. *I learned—in time—how to recycle my losses into opportnities*

Regina Louise
September 2nd, 2016

Prologue

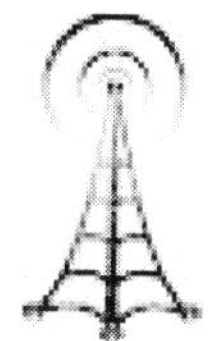

Transcript

NPR Tavis Smiley
July 1, 2003 | NPR Tavis Smiley
Interview: Regina Louise discusses growing up in foster care.

Host: TAVIS SMILEY
Time: 9:00-10:00 AM

Billie Holiday (singing): *So the Bible says and it still is true, Mama may have, Papa may have, but God bless the child that's got his own, that's got his own…*

Tavis Smiley: From NPR in Los Angeles, I'm Tavis Smiley. Regina Louise is a foster care advocate and frequent speaker at foster care conventions across the country. Regina Louise, now a mother and a successful entrepreneur tells her harrowing and triumphant tale in "*Somebody's Someone: A Memoir.*" Earlier I spoke with Regina about her book and asked her what it felt like to be unwanted as a child.

Tavis: Welcome to the show, Regina

Louise: Thank you, Tavis. It feels good to be here.

Tavis: Jonathan, put the cover of this book back up for me, if you will, right quick. The cover of this book features a Black child with an umbrella covering her face. And there is a reason why we see this particular photo, rather than what could have, and perhaps should have been a photo of you during your foster care years. So, why this photo?

Louise: Well, as they say Tavis, “A rolling stone gathers no moss.” As a child, I didn’t stay in any particular home long enough to have photos taken.

Tavis: I think, for obvious reasons now, it tells a story about your experience when you can’t even find a photo, to use on the cover of your book.

Louise: You’re gonna make me cry. (Laughs.)

Tavis *(laughs)*: I don’t wanna make you cry. And I’m curious about your experiences, because for someone who’s had to live through so many different homes, and institutions, the system wasn’t kind to you.

Louise: It is amazing when I stop and think about it, or write about it in this case.

Tavis: Yes, indeed that’s an amazing story?

Tavis: I want you to take a minute. Take a minute, and collect yourself, then, if you don’t mind tell me about your experiences…

Book One

Etiology

"It's in relationships where we get wounded, and it is in relationships where we get healed, Gina," my therapist, Lainey told me back in 1998 while I sat in her cozy San Francisco corner office where I'd shelled out one hundred and sixty dollars for fifty minutes of talk therapy; I desperately chewed-up our time together hoping to save, retrieve and or gather up what was left of my raggedy sense of self. A decade past emancipating from foster care I was confounded by the weight I still carried, the baggage of feeling unwanted, unavailable—to my self mostly—the emotional malaise that seemed to put a choke-hold on the little bit of hope I was suddenly dying to hold onto. The well-worn sofa held me like I wished my daddy would have, all velvety and warm, my feet planted, firmly, on the ground in front of me, my hands rested on my thighs palm-side up, and only the Lord knew that I'd come begging for a blessing that day, a holding onto, a something to make it feel like mine was a life worth living.

My life had reached a point where I was starting to walk around like a shell-shocked soldier; I couldn't sleep, eat or continue to find meaning in the everydayness of every day, and other variables, such as grief and loss presented themselves, weighed in on my bearings—memories for which I had no language for. I felt estranged from myself. Lost. My son, at that time, brought me much pleasure from being his mother, and I guessed the same protective factors that motivated me to take the managing of my own life, into my own hands as a child, were also the contributing aspects that informed me enough to know: it wasn't my child's job to save me; that was my work to do, to find the resources, people, coping mechanisms to take my life back from the horrors of my childhood and early adulthood experiences. I needed to turn my devastation into my motivation.

Lainey, eyes locked on mine, mirrored my breathing, my body movements, my affect, as she held the space allowing for one loss after another, like Lazarus, to resurrect from the dark and make their way into the light. "Gina, can you tell me your first memory of your mother?" Lainey asked within a month of our first meeting. It was an innocent enough question but for the life of me I came up with nothing. Nothing, that is, except the feeling that the room was spinning. Fast. As if I was suddenly caught in a category five tornado and without warning I was spinning backwards into a place and time where things that had happened had no edges or borders. It felt like complete chaos.

Events blended into one another in ways that left me bewildered. Confused. As if the mere mention of my mother threatened to melt the resolve I thought I'd acquired up till then, sending me spiraling, and cavorting back through memories frozen in a darkness so frighteningly real I could, again, feel terror pump through my chest as though my life were at risk, again.

The therapy, meant to be *self-directed*, many times opened the door for pieces of the past to slip through. On occasion, I'd have a memory so startlingly clear I'd find myself sitting on the front porch of the house I grew up in. Just waiting. Peach cob bler cooling on a side rail, chili beans simmering on the stove behind me. Sometimes Big Mama, my first caretaker showed up, without wearing her dentures, gumming my name like she was right there beside me, "Ghee-na," she'd whisper. The taste of her fried catfish and coleslaw made my mouth water. At other times, my mother, Ruby, by way of a whiff of her Pall Mall's, or the sound of her full body laugh visited me; and from my father I might've received a glimpse of his nose and the hair that hung from it like dried pussywillow, and how it moved up, and down when he spoke. I was grateful that Lainey never pushed, only asked the powerful questions meant to probe, gently shift my understanding of the relationships I had or didn't have, and then she'd step back to allow room for whatever showed up.

Eventually, I consented to trying Eye Movement Desensitization and Reprocessing (EMDR), anytime Big Mama came around. I used it to process many of my memories, but the thoughts of Big Mama, and my inability to articulate what she meant to me brought out a grief in me that could knock me into a spell of speechlessness for days on end. Lainey would ask me to find a memory, to follow it until a feeling would emerge. Once I had the memory, or feeling we'd discuss how I felt, what was happening, and at the moment I'd collide with the unsayable Lainey would stop me. She'd put up two fingers to my eye-level and move them back and forth like windshield wipers and I'd follow her movements sharing what I could till eventually, the feeling of sadness or overwhelm would subside. I'd feel better able to think about my past in ways that allowed me to remember without terror, hopelessness, I became better able to manage the shame.

Unlike "all the king's horses, and all the king's men," over time I learned how to sit with those recollections, how to recognize and diffuse those triggers one little step at a time. I used whatever modality I could get my hands on: acupuncture, massage, special tinctures to calm my nerves, cranial sacral release, yoga, hypnotherapy. From each discipline I took what I could and used it as the mortar to stitch my life back together again, patchwork it in such a way that reordered space, so that I could locate myself in time. Time and time again though, I found myself marooned in my own awareness that although I'd done all the right things: grew myself up, accepted that my rejections were not personal; made it a practice to follow the *Golden Rule*: I *still* had to learn that nothing could guarantee I'd get what I really wanted: relations who privileged my need to be a daughter, sister, cousin, grand-daughter, aunt, or partner. A good mother. My need to have someone stay.

In almost all of my relationships—today—my ability to stay, do the work: confront the wounding in tandem with a loved one, to heal the generational scars left by known and unspeakable traumas alike, remains in process.

Side Step, Push Back

Even now I am impervious to the jab meant to silence, demean, or deny the connection I seek and as a result I give too much, too quickly, turn the other cheek habitually terrified I'll be rejected, once again, marked for being *too big*, or *too mouthy* or just more than anyone will ever want anything to do with.

She's just too much.

I allow others to side-step, push back, even obliterate my personal borders because I'm afraid that if I stand up for myself—this time—If I defend against the limiting beliefs of who or what I "should be," given the gender, class and circumstances I was born into, that somehow, still, I will sabotage my efforts to fit in, stay put, belong to anyone worth more than a pinch of salt.

In this *now* life, the one where I am sometimes a lover, an on-and-off-again-friend, voice for the unclaimed, a fictive sister to more folks than I can keep up with: I tend to be overly concerned that these alliances' too, will cast me off, and out. Sometimes I hear that I am "too therapized," and I imagine what is left unspoken is that my being once feral, and now rehabilitated, equals hypervigilence for the tiniest infractions. I have a high appreciation for keeping things just and evenhanded.

She's just too much.

So, as if fueled by an unnatural impulse to gratify, I easily met out 'Yes' when I mean to say 'No.' I take up far too much space providing, allowing, accepting, backpedaling the moment I sense I am vulnerable to rejection.

I charge trauma as the ringleader of these reactions, the triumphant instigator that has no mercy for the destruction it lays waste to. Once detonated, some traumas have the effect of deregulating the body's natural defense mechanisms. Sometimes I:

- Freeze when I should fight;
- Run when I should freeze,
- Stay when I should take flight.

By 2003, my teenaged son was a thriving scholar-athlete in one of the country's top boarding schools. I had two "Best of the Bay" hair salons under my belt, clients booked out ten weeks in advance, a partner I adored, and an apricot poodle named Wynona. I loved that dog like a twin.* In so many ways my life was good. I had much to be grateful for, and I was.

---

*Noni (as I called her), and I took second place in a Bay-to-Barkers owner and pet look alike contest. I'm certain that had it not been for the fifth grader and her blond-haired Cocker spaniel—they did actually look far too much alike to deny the fact—Noni and I would've taken first place.

However, my time was over-promised to far too many, and soon it became overwhelmingly difficult to deliver on the things that were most important; relationships, career, familial commitments. The stress of it all put an uncalled-for amount of strain on an already taxed situation. So, on an honor handshake, I handed-off my house, the first home I ever owned, first symbol of stability I've ever had, the house I purchased from the hardscrabble work of cutting, styling and blow drying hair.

I was the first and only African American business owner on Berkeley's upscale *Fourth Street* shopping destination. My partner Stevie Ann, and I worked long, grueling hours to put *Keter Salon* on it's feet, to service our clients with the latest and best hair products, we hired talented stylists who were dedicated to their trade. We aspired to create a communal space where emerging artist could hang their art, a cool joint where pet owners brought their dogs in dressed to the nines in costumes for photo shoots that helped raise funds for the Berkeley *S.P.C.A.*

Local designers displayed and sold their wares at salon-sponsored trunk shows all the while chomping on fried chicken, and sipping on champagne in order to give foster children trips to *Build-a-Bear Workshop*, and dinner at *Goat Hill Pizza*.

We were "all-in" Stevie and I was. I cared a lot for that woman. Most of all she was my friend, my family. She was a pretty woman, Stevie Ann. Athletic. Thin. On any given day she'd give Demi Moore a run for her money, and win.

So, I had no hesitations when Stevie Anne said: "You'll always have a home, with me, Gina," I believed her when she said "Neither you or Michael will ever be homeless." She knew the chords to strum, she'd baptized herself in the tune of my want. Out of honor and what I thought family was supposed to mean: transparency, the ability to have difficult conversations, love and honor.

I signed-over both hair salons I'd scouted out the locations for during my lunch breaks, and arranged and managed contractors for. I'd filed all the permits and licenses for those businesses. "This is an emotional time. You're writing through a lot of trauma, you're not as present as I need you to be, and you're not able to meet your clients needs," she said. "Let me handle your affairs, we're family." There was that word. The password to my Achilles heel. What I wouldn't have given at that moment to understand the value of other folks' projections. How to know the difference between best intentions and ego-driven actions? How I wished I'd understood how ever-so-easily it was to let someone know what *they* were going through, from *our* perspective and the weight and validity that both speaker and listener give to one another in the name of love.

Stevie stopped returning my phone calls. Emails. Texts. She had everything: businesses. House. First dog I ever had, and loved. My writing studio. I let her keep it. All of it. If I was going to have to choose between the reclamation of myself, and playing small in order to be loved: Then I was willing to lose it all, for me.

Nevertheless. I am still quick to grant second, third and fourth chances to folks who say they love me, will never leave me, *we will always be family*, they say as they leave, anyway. Trauma is a feeder road to never knowing what will happen next. It oftentimes shatters my ability to stay fastened to any one person for any real length of time. And even when I do, attachment is insecure at best. I'm never quite able to fully recognize to what, or to whom I belong.

Recovering myself would become a life-long practice.

I've learned, that who I am today is a direct mark of the disturbances I have had in my developmental climb towards an actualized being. I have endured: rejection, loss, abandonment. Openly.

I am a brown-skinned woman who was born out of wedlock, misborn a bastard. And I repeat: none of these facts were ever intended for me, or directed at me as though they were meant to be personal. Life, in and of itself is what I make of it, how I am able to interpret, or reimagine it in such a way that makes each day an unprecedented testimony to what is possible.

Trauma, and its co-conspirators; shock, denial, shame, anxiety, anger, hopelessness, the inability to cope with daily life, and the granddaddy of them all Post Traumatic Stress Disorder (PTSD) all join forces to rob us of a chance to allow our God-given personalities to come into their own. Much is required to remain stuck, or maybe even frozen in a state of painful unconsciousness. To me, this is what trauma demands: a certain tending to, a sacrificing that gives nothing back but more of the same emptiness, more of the same inability to live this one life to its fullest. Although my body has kept score of all the hardships I've experienced, and has archived them in places that're hard for me to recognize, I've learned to be grateful to my traumas. When they arrive, I do what I can to befriend them, to reimagine them as long lost children, tugging at the hemline of my awareness to be seen, heard. Found.

But until I was able to understand, more fully, what was being asked of me I saw trauma differently. I saw it as something that begged for my complete devastation, and in many cases it wasn't willing to take anything less.

Taxonomy

My mothers' abandonment, was a tributary of her mother's leaving, was a repercussion of her mother's mother's disappearing, and all the streams lead back to the river of these women's refutations:

1. being born black.
2. poor.
3. invisible.
4. the trauma of belonging is congenital.

As a child, in 1972, where I lived in a sharecroppers shack on land that was handed down from generations of black hands, and black bodies toiling away beneath the roiling Texas sun picking cotton, blueberries and shovel-whipping rattlesnakes the size of a three-ply Manila tug-of-war rope; I learned that to stand up for myself—in relationships—was to risk being seen as troublesome, spiked good with the Devil's blood, the whistleblower. I was dangerous. I was to be rid of.

Say another word and I'll beat the black off you right where you stand, were Lula Mae's words—the eldest foster child of Rosetta and Newt Cavanaugh also known as Big Mama and Daddy Newt my mother's keepers, and eventually mine too—Lula's threats, booming with detestation and spitefulness spewed from her mouth on a daily basis because she made it clear how *f—d up* it was that our mother had abandoned my sister Cynthia and

I to be taken care of by folks who didn't want to be *bothered with the burden in the first place.* I was ten years old and believed that if I made a wish upon a star, the wish would come true. I also believed Lula's threats of terrorization. We all did.

I wished like heck, I didn't live there anymore.

I'd witnessed first-hand how the adults in my world did business, how their intimidations were never idle, and how satisfied they seemed to collect on the promise of extracting recompense from the rear end of the one who'd committed the unforeseen offense. Expectations were hidden, like landmines; we didn't know where they were until they exploded in our faces. Oops. "Your behind is mine now," is how Lula Mae usually put it. As if it wasn't humiliating enough to get it wrong, as if that fact alone, that we'd shamed ourselves, wasn't payment enough. The worst part about self-hate—in my humbled estimation—is that far too many times the self doesn't even know it's *itself* it hates, and not the one it bullies, not the one it takes the rage out on.

On several occasions I'd watched as my sister Cynthia failed to protest against the accusations that she was a lying, conniving, nobody's child. That she was bad for wanting more than our caregivers were willing to give her. That even though she was Big Mama's favorite, and could do no wrong, when it came to Lula Mae Bledsoe, Big Mama's eldest foster child; favoritism gave way to a hard-row-to-hoe, and my sister became a target of Lula's own backwoods ideologies of a child's fate should the rod be spared.

I listened as my soft-spoken sister took her time—to buy time—while she slipped the elastic waistband of her shorts down the length of coffee-colored legs, the fabric etching ashy marks into her dry skin. She'd strip down to her nakedness only to be wet-down with a water hose, and whipped, again and again with an extension cord, or a *Hot Wheels* track for stashing away a soiled sanitary napkin, a mayonnaise sandwich, a matching pair of lace trimmed socks, or anything she wanted to keep secret beneath the mattress of the bed I shared with her. Afterwards.

- I was the one who held her hand through that unnecessary suffering
- I was the one who gently dropped the Mercurochrome onto her raw flesh, careful not to let the tip of the dabber touch the open wound, staining the pink spots red which over a few days would fade to brown
- I was the one who hoped against hope my mother Ruby would show up at any minute and do the same to Lula.

My sister was the one who'd introduced me to Mercurochrome; there were many times she'd had to use it on me.

I had a front row seat for the violence and terror that played out right in front of my childhood eyes. Fist fights over money, women and the men who had plenty of both but refused to shell out a cent for the children they sired out of wedlock which left a trail of bastards a mile long for anyone who gave a *Good-Goddamned* to come along and collect us for the promise of a few dollars here, a block of government issued cheese there. Love was never an interchangeable commodity.

While reading the newspaper in 1972, when I was ten years old, I came across a notice about a shooting that had occurred the previous night, somewhere near South Sixth Street in a motel whose name I've long since forgotten. The information stated that when police officers arrived on the scene a one Ruby Carmichael, a black female of South Austin had been shot in the lower abdomen by the girlfriend of an unidentified male. The victim, had come through surgery, was in critical condition, but was expected to survive. I couldn't swallow back the terror of that moment fast enough.

What I knew then: My mother's name was Ruby Carmichael and that it was common knowledge she had a penchant for other people's property, that she didn't want no one, or no thing that was trifling or incapable of feeding her need for extreme chaos washed back with a fifth of scotch or any other malted whiskey, any other woman's boyfriend. Husband. The gun-toting girlfriend had accused my mother of stealing her man. My mother, in return, chastised the woman for being unqualified to hold onto her own man, and refused to take the blame for something the girlfriend seemed to bring onto herself. The woman shot my mother at point blank range. Unlike my sister, my mother stood up for what she believed. Right or wrong.

I loved our mother for the legendary proportions her behaviors took on, her fiery ways of getting what she wanted. She acted out the way I wanted to but was too young to do so. I did not understand her not using that same fire to want us.

Although that was not the first trauma my mother had experienced; it was the one that would catapult me even deeper into a childhood chocked-full of adverse experiences. Nothing would ever feel safe again.

A year or so later, on the day, Lula Mae attempted to beat the black off me started out as an ordinary day. I awoke with the expectation of attending the carnival that had taken up residence in the Safe way parking lot four blocks from where I lived. Some of my classmates were going to be there as well, and we'd hope to meet up at the cakewalk. My intention was to win a cake and share it with my friends. I was cranked-up.

Lula called me into the house from the curb I'd been standing on while rocking her teething, toddler, Ella. The baby seemed to prefer the sound of motor vehicles passing over asphalt to anything else, since it kept her quiet so that Lula could stay tuned to her new favorite daytime drama: *The Young and the Restless*. I gave the child what she wanted: a half hour or so of rocking her on my hip while we watched car after car pass by. I handed Ella off to Dorothy Jean, the traitor who also lived on our property and the one who'd told Lula that I'd stood in the middle of the street playing dodge-the-car with Ella. Such an act would've certified me as undeniably insane, and the symptoms of my senselessness would've shown up (I imagined) far earlier than that day. But somehow, Lula failed to consider that I'd never been that close to crazy in all my life.

Lula wasn't one to miss out on an opportunity to course correct a wrongdoing, nor an occasion to "take it outta your behind."

The cut-off water hose whistled through the air as she laid into my body with a force I'd not known before. Fury burned across her face in waves of fine ridges, and thick folds of skin until her mouth became a sinkhole of rage. Lula blew fire. She claimed that since I was one-part devil and the other part my mother it was her duty to beat the desires of both out of me along with the blackness of my skin. Lula was black. Folger's Coffee black with a dollop of cream. I understood, then, that to be black was bad, to be black was just cause to be obliterated, to be black was a blasphemy that not even God could protect against. I was on my own. I made a pact with God anyway, that should Lula beat me again that it would be a sign from Him that I should leave.

I wasn't my sister. I wasn't some "still waters run deep" kind of girl too afraid to tell anyone how I felt about the way they treated me, to afraid to be my own savior. I heard, nearly everyday, how much of a "bull in a China cabinet I was," and how I needed to be more like my sister. I told myself that I wasn't about to let Lula hate me to death with a whip. So, like I imagined my mother would have done had she faced Lula down, after blows upon blows of her battering my flesh, I turned on Lula and caught the cut-off water hose in mid air. My hand stung. I didn't care.

"I didn't do nothing wrong," I screamed at Lula. For a moment we stood arms raised above our heads holding on with all our strength to that cut-off green water hose, we both had to keep one another away from the other. "You ain't gonna be a nothing," Lula Mae screamed as Big Mama plowed through the door. "Just like your no 'count mama, a nothing."

Make good on the pact you made with God. Keep your word. She hit you again, it's your sign, the one from Him: (God.) Time to go. She tried to kill you. Leave. Now. Run. You can do this. Run. Don't look back. Run. Don't stop till you know you'll be safe. Run.

I ran from 2423 South Fifth Street, for my life: over the juniper shrubs, through the wall of cypress trees that shielded the front of the house from the street, onto the footpath that lead past the 7-Eleven at the corner where my street, the only place I'd ever known as *home*, crossed West Oltorf. "You ain't gonna be a nothing..." Lula Mae screamed, and her words hissed at the backs of my heels.

I circled back over Oak Crest Street, high-tailed it through the parking lot of San Jose Catholic Church where, on many an Ash Wednesday, I'd stood and watched through the windows, as the Priest, in their colorful robes, and large white hands, made the sign of the crucifixion in what I imagined were cigarette ashes onto the center of people's foreheads. Oh how I envied them and coveted the protection of their God; I ran, my flesh wounds whipping against the heat of that late August night, alongside Juanita Avenue until I crossed South 1st Street, near my elementary school, Molly Dawson, and I didn't stop until I reached my best friend Sonya Perez' house.

"gone…be a nothing."

For God so loved the world that He gave His only begotten Son and Whosoever shall believe shall not parish but have everlasting life.

— John 3:16

Repeat until you can breathe again, until you forget the throbbing, the sting, the pain, until you no longer want to beat the black off Lula Mae one thundering blow after another.

Blam! Blam! Blam! Blam!

I made a solemn promise to live long enough so that one day I could tell on Lula Mae. I didn't know who I'd tell. It just made me feel better to think I could, would tell someone. Even as a child I knew it wasn't right to want to beat a child until their flesh was gone, until they couldn't speak, couldn't move, couldn't breathe. I needed Lula to know that my spirit belonged to me, that she had no right to think I should take what she gave me and not ask why. I'd spend the rest of my life glad for that moment, in complete gratitude to the strength and fortitude and act of self-compassion I was able to give myself that day. It would take a lifetime for me to understand the profundity of that moment of choosing me.

My mother, Ruby, paid a high price to belong to no one, in the end. According to legend, in 1946, my mother was found sitting on the floor in the middle of the kitchen in the house she lived in with her mother, sister and the ghost of her two dead brothers. Her mother lay there, four days dead. Minnie was my first and real grandmother's name. My sister would reveal this story to me six decades after the fact.

My mother was three years old. Her sister, Toni five years older, was holding their mother's slack hand. As the sayings go: my mother's mother—my grandmother—drank a bottle of lye on account that rheumatic fever took her two sons from her. The neighbor and family friend, Rosetta Cavanaugh, happened upon the situation, took my mother and her sister in.

While staying at the Cavanaugh compound Rosetta reached out to one of my mother's uncles and informed him of the girls' loss, and the circumstances of how she came to have them and shortly thereafter the veteran came on the regular to visit Minnie's girls.

*Po' thangs wit' out no mama.**

He took quickly to my mother, as many men had, with her copper-penny red hair, skin the color of a sun-kissed Georgia peach, her pillow soft lips.

*The commentaries of folks who always had something to say.

My mother loved to bathe, and evidently her uncle Alfred loved bathing her. His hand to soap, hand to cloth, hand to skin water ritual lead to the incomprehensible, and on the cusp of turning thirteen my mother gave birth to her first child, my sister, her second cousin. By what metric can the damage that trauma initiated be measured?

When my mother gave birth to Cynthia she passed on to her the gift of a photographic memory, the ability, at ten, to draw *Tippy* from the back of a *Richie Rich* comic book and warranted a visit from an *Art Instruction School* representative. Cynthia became Rosetta Cavanaugh's girl.

For the short and intermittent moments, I spent with her, my mother, she was highly unpredictable. Without sign, signal or sound her moods slipped from her in bites, and fits and scratches, she not only kicked but also brandished a 44-magnum pistol (always pointed at my sister), and threw firebricks at the hood of her male friend's brand new car. She slammed doors and threatened, "I brought you into this world, and I'll take your black-█ out!" Classic. Ruby.

When she wasn't working eleven at night to seven in the morning at Seton Memorial Hospital with the elderly, or in some private residence "cleaning old-█ white people's ███," she was bed-ridden from migraines, cigarette hangovers and way too much scotch. She could barely stand the sight of her own fool self.

And even to this day, I'm not sure I'd recognize my mother if she were to pass me on the street. Trauma, like my mother, was sometimes a self-serving narcissist.

I've never known the exact date, or conditions under which my mother thought it was a good idea to leave me, and or my sister in the care of people who thought it fitting for a grown man—Uncle Alfred—to indulge himself on the innocence of an adolescent girl. Like so many perpetrators he then snuck away in the night. I imagine my young mother did the best she could with what she had, and at the time her best probably dictated that we would be better off, my sister and I, with the devils we knew as opposed to the one's she didn't.

I—now—am better able to understand how we were all haphazardly stitched together, back then, by the harrowing consequences of what we didn't know.

Book Two

My Father Was Almost Famous

His album *I Love You More and More* was released in the summer of 1974. It was expected to soar to the top of the R&B charts. The great Gene Page, who'd worked with The Four Tops, Barbra Streisand, and Marvin Gaye, arranged many of the songs on Tom Brock's debut LP. The album had four songs on the A-side and four more on the B-side, and the *Love Unlimited Orchestra* backs him up. I can't imagine what it must've felt like to have one hundred and fifty musicians show up just for me. Tom Brock had it good. I suppose.

There he sits, my father, on the cover of his album, on a beige settee with embroidery stitching, wearing a red velvet tuxedo jacket with black lapels over a white turtleneck.* Smooth. An oversized ficus tree looms in the background and a chandelier dangles overhead. He holds a glass of red wine in one hand, although I never remember him having a drink, while the other touched the arm of a dark-skinned woman. She is not my mother. Their eyes, like the lighting in the room, are lowered, smoldering. Locked.

---

* I haggled with an aggressive seller on EBay for nearly a week in order to get a copy of the CD. In the end I paid seventy-five dollars to hear my father's voice, again.

He wrote hit songs for Glodean James, Gloria Scott, and for The Sultan of Soul himself, Mr. Barry White, and Barry produced Tom's album. He played the piano, my father, faster than Jerry Lee Lewis and taught himself classical guitar. His lead song "There Is Nothing in This World That Can Stop Me from Loving You" debuted on the pop charts at #90. Yet his album was a dud. It would be another thirty years before that title song would have its day, courtesy of Jay-Z who sampled it into his blockbuster hit *GirlzGirlzGirlz.* The royalty checks I—now—get from BMI are the most I've ever received from my father.

He lived in Los Angeles back then. The Westside. He also kept residence in Richmond, California. And in 1975, when I was twelve, I went to live with him in a bungalow in Richmond, with his Norwegian wife, Nadine, and their three children. By then he'd lost everything that mattered to him; his record deal, his relationship with Barry. His mind.

Their children; two girls, and a boy all had their own bedrooms in that little house on Downer Avenue. I slept on the couch in the living room. Its arms were frayed.

I lasted nearly two months.

My father was a "high-yellow" black boy. Eighteen. My mother was seventeen. As the story goes, Tom met my mother, Ruby, at the high school she'd dropped out of in order to take care of my sister who was nearly five years-old. I'd first met Tom when I was nine or ten, the exact age I could not say, because things were chaotic back then.

That time, Ruby had sent me from Jacksonville North Carolina to stay with my father because her live-in boyfriend, Mr. Benny, asked me to let him touch my nipples. He wanted to do to me what the "middle-finger" stood for. He chewed toothpicks in between his requests.

One night, after I had been in Richmond a month and a half, I wanted to hear my mama's voice. I missed how she called me "Gina-girl." "Gina-girl," she'd say, and I'd stop whatever it was I was doing and run to her. Quick-like. Given that I lived mostly with Big Mama, with only brief and random trials of living with Ruby to see if we could gel, I wanted to make every word, look, touch, and the-way-she-called-my-name, stick for as long as it could. I had to talk to her.

But Nadine, Tom's Norwegian wife who I sometimes imagined was a witch with her long black hair, and those eyes that sunk into her face surrounded by dark circles, she controlled all access to communication in the house, including the kitchen phone. She said I didn't have permission to call my mother, given I had no money to pay a phone bill.

Should I Call My Mother?

I took one of the kids' *Magic Eight Ball* and shook it, and shook it, and shook to determine whether or not I should call my mother? Anyway.

I Wanted, I Wished, I Dug

I snuck into my father's and his wife's bedroom, which was "off-limits." There, atop one of the matching bedside tables, sat a pink princess telephone. I'd never seen anything like that phone in my life.

Tucked between the nightstand and the side of the bed, I slowly lifted the receiver. My fingertips fit perfectly into the grayish, indented squares. The *boop boop boop* of the keypad excited me. The phone rang twice. I was seconds away from hearing my mama.

"Hi, Ruby. It's me—" "Get off my phone!" Nadine hollered from the kitchen. "Hey now, Gin—" my mama said just before the line clicked dead. I slammed the receiver down. "You cain't do that!" I yelled into Nadine's face.

She had a way of staying silent, her eyes fearless. She was a school principal; my desire for my mother was forever in detention.

For a short while, I curled up like a prawn on that scratchy-to-the-touch sofa, and pleaded with God to send my mother to me.

> "Dear God, please send my mother to me.
> I don't belong here, with these people. They don't

> like me, and I don't care so much for them. Please. Please. Send me my mother."

I wanted to swim in the White Shoulders Eau de Perfume she slathered on.

I wanted her to never stop calling me "Gina-girl. Gina-girl. Gina-girl."

I wanted the odor of Pall Mall's on her breath mixed with watered down scotch to waft over me just once more before whichever one of us died.

That night, I walked straight out of the front door and marched the more than thirty city blocks to the big laundromat on Rheem Ave. Whenever my friends and I ditched school—Downer Elementary, which was right around the corner—we'd go to the laundromat and race up and down the aisles in the laundry baskets. I always won.

I waited for the last woman to pull her clothes from the dryers, and when everyone had left, just before closing, I laid the upper half of my body inside to stay warm.

I stared at the speckled black and white enamel dryer drum as though it was the night sky. I looked for the big and little dipper, hoping to wish upon them that my father would snap-off on Nadine for my leaving. He'd make her sit down and write:

I'm sorry, Regina.
I'm sorry, Regina.
I'm sorry, Regina, a thousand times, until she meant it.
I wished that at any moment my father would come looking for me, and once he found me, I'd agree to go home with him.

I wished that I could let him touch me, carefully, and in so doing, I wouldn't break, or be ruined, or even get accused of being a prick tease, like Ruby had said concerning Mr. Benny. "Prick tease" is what she called me. I had no idea what such a thing meant, prick tease. Anyway, at the time I knew better than to let what she said hurt my feelings, it wouldn't have mattered: I wasn't afraid to stand up to anyone except, Ruby. I couldn't take it knowing that she'd have no reservations to pulling a gun on me, or cursing me out. I convinced myself she meant no harm by saying what she had said.

If he came, my father, I promised myself to let him take my hand, and hold it, if only long enough to lead me to the car, buckle me in, and tell me it was natural to want my mother, even if she didn't want me. I would've wanted the truth. I needed the truth.

I dug donut holes from the garbage can of the bakery next door. Sitting on the bench out front, I removed any trace of mold or dirt and popped the sweet balls into my mouth. Every now and again, I imagined my father's metallic-green Lincoln Continental with the suicide doors driving by, and just as he would catch sight of me, park and then kill the engine and head towards me I'd make him disappear. Psyche. I'd go back to eating the donut holes.

I Held My Head High

The next morning, I crawled from behind the bakery's garbage cans where I'd slept through the night. Hungry, I headed to school. I loved school. Even though I got into trouble, a lot, for reading ahead, or solving a math problem without showing how I worked it out, and yelling the answer out loud. At lunch time, in the cafeteria, I pretended to be the *Six Million-Dollar Man* and I cut in the food line. A boy my same height poked me from behind. He asked me to move.

"Make me," I said. Another boy, standing in front of me also turned around; he was the twin of the boy behind me. Despite their talking smack, and weak attempts to push me out of the line, I managed to get a tray, plate of food, milk, a butter knife, and fork.

I held my head high as I handed the cashier my yellow "free lunch" ticket and headed to a table in the middle of the cafeteria. Out of nowhere, one of the twins pushed me. I recovered my footing in just enough time to turn and slam the tray into his face.

I fought both of them.

Then I ran. I became Lindsey Wagner. I was the *Bionic Woman.* There was no one I could not defeat.

An hour or so later, I arrived at my friend Mary Cosentiniano's house. She always left her bedroom window open, just in case I ever got in a pickle and needed a place. I didn't go the night before because I wasn't about to wear out my welcome. I knew better. Also, I knew that I wouldn't be able to stay long, and I'd promised myself to use her room only if I had no other choice.

It was good, her house with its mother and father, two sisters and an older brother who played drums in the garage. He let Mary sing backup for me while I gave my best Stevie Nicks' impression of Rhiannon. Jimmy drummed along with Nick Fleetwood. Jimmy was going to be somebody in a real band. Me too. I was going to have a solo career like Karen Carpenter, or Gladys Knight, or maybe even Diana Ross.

Hanging out with the Cosentiniano's was better than wasting time trying to stay out of the way at Nadine's and Tom's with their three kids and not nearly enough room for "his bastard." Not to mention that, by that time, Tom had begun to hallucinate. He imagined the government had unleashed wild animals in the neighborhood. Sometimes he went hunting, bringing back half carcasses large and small, and after cleaning them he'd hang them to line dry in the kitchen. At Mary's they all sat around a table at the same hour every night and ate meat pulled from styrofoam and saran wrap.

The mother, her bushy hair always flat on one side from her daily naps, would bring plates of food and set them between a vase of dandelions and a Tupperware salt and pepper set. I loved the gold "P" and "S" on the slender-waist bottles and swore to myself that one day I too would buy a set from myself when I threw my first Tupperware party.

They'd all eat as if the salad, and gnocchi smothered in meat gravy was the best meal they'd ever eaten. The way they talked between bites, and laughed with mouths full of food and hands whirring and flapping this way and that, made the hush between my own kin deafening.

Shortly after that phone episode, my father received a call from a woman claiming she'd recently given birth to his son. Tom moved back to Los Angeles.

I had nowhere else to go.

Garbage Bag Caught On The Windowsill

In the spring of 1976. I'd already lived, for two months, with a friend of mine from sixth grade. I asked my friend to ask her mother, Mrs. Bushfield if I could come and live with them and the woman agreed to take care of me while Tom was away in Los Angeles. I came home after school one day and the doors were locked. I could feel it was time to go.

"You in there?" I knocked on the backdoor of an unkempt house. I wore Ditto's Jeans, a white T-shirt with a red glitter rose and raggedy red Converse sneakers. "Mrs. Bushfield? Mrs. Bushfield if you in there I just come for my stuff!"
No answer.

I peeked through the kitchen windows. It was clear. I dragged a garbage can over to the window, stood on it, and pushed my way inside the kitchen. I had to move fast. I had no idea when Mrs. Bushfield might return. One after the other I searched through the kitchen drawers until I found a Glad garbage bag. I'd lived long enough with strangers to know, in my bones, the things they didn't say but would want to beat me half to death for if I didn't somehow magically know. I was safe if I stuck to:

1) Never using the Lord's name in vain
2) Saying: Goddamit
3) Saying: Lord have mercy
4) Saying: For God's sake
5) Saying: Lord knows
6) Never asking for anything, other than what was given
7) Never even *thinking* about bringing up my own heart break
8) Never. Ever. Get so comfortable to think I have a right "to anything in this here house."

I headed for the stairs. All two hundred plus pounds of Mrs. Bushfield raged around the corner towards me. My sixth grade best friend's mother, the woman my father had agreed to pay for keeping me, placed herself between me and both the front and the back doors. I had no way out. "Little good for nothin'! Ain't nothin' up in here belonging to you. Give me my bag back, now!"

Mrs. Bushfield snatched me by my hair. I needed that bag. I held on. We fought and she smashed my face into the corner of a wall. The two of us fell to the floor. Mrs. Bushfield tried to pull my clothes from my body; my pants, t-shirt. I kicked at Mrs. Bushfield. Mrs. Bushfield grabbed hold of my left foot and attempted to remove my shoe. "These is my shoes Mrs. Bushfield! They mine! My father, Tom, gave me the money for 'em." The more I thrashed, the more I kicked, the tighter Mrs. Bushfield held on. I used the base of the banister to hold on while doing anything I could to get free from that woman. "Yo' so-called daddy ain't paid for a thang up in here, freeloader! You not even worth the price of these here shoes."

Finally, free, I ran up the stairs and locked myself inside the small bedroom with it's two twin beds, six-drawer dresser, and closet full of everything and anything Anica could think to ask for. They were "doing the good Lord's work," by giving me a bed even though my “no ‘count” father had reneged on his payment agreements.

Using a chair, I barricaded the door. Mrs. Bushfield scampered up the stairs. Whatever I could grab, I crammed into the ripped garbage bag, and the back of my pants pockets; a mood ring, a cigarette, a plastic baggie holding the tissue that held the last kiss my mother had given me.

Mrs. Bushfield pummeled the door. I Shuddered.

Mrs. Bushfield’ pounding became increasingly frantic. “I’m a kill you.” Mrs. Bushfield screamed. I picked up a phone receiver and dialed the Operator. “Lord knows you nothing but a ingrate!” Mrs. Bushfield screamed. “Operator! Can you connect me to the police department?” I whispered, watching the door, and listening for movement.

Boom!

The door gave way. Mrs. Bushfield rushed into the room towards me. I disappeared out of the window, and jumped two stories, leaving the garbage bag caught on the windowsill.

Until The Sun Towed Daylight Into The Sky

Sunday, May 2, 1976, was my thirteenth birthday. I awoke in a two-window room, in Martinez, California. The windows were chicken-wired shut and reinforced with nuts and bolts. The Edgar Children's Shelter. It was an orphanage. By orphanage I don't mean a Victorian Era-Dickensian poorhouse like in *Oliver Twist*. This wasn't the *Annie* version either. Edgar Children's Shelter was a county-maintained receiving center that accepted displaced children from all over the San Francisco Bay Area on a twenty-four-hour basis.

It was a one-story ranch-style dwelling on an acre of scorched earth. The county had kept painting the clapboard building a yellowish-beige till it took on the color of pale phlegm. Even though Edgar was a place to deposit unwanted children, the county had done its best to blend the institutionalized site into the middle-class neighborhood by adding an eight-foot cyclone fence with cedar slats that surrounded the property, shielding it from the outside world, as did Juniper Bushes, which smelled like cat piss. A worn American flag waved from an equally tired flagpole.

I had arrived in the middle of the night. Two police officers led me from the backseat of a squad car into the intake room where a bald-headed man, who looked as if he'd just swallowed the moon, Mr. Porter, processed my arrival. Sweat dripped down his forehead and temples, and his belly pressed hard against his shirt, his elastic waistband, and his desk. "Do you have any next of kin?" he asked. I shook my head no. "Do you know your father's whereabouts?" I shook my head no. "What about your mother?

What about my mother? I'd wanted to ask Mr. Porter. What is it, exactly; you want to know about her? Had I the gumption, the pluck, or sass that I normally packed around with me like a bag full of buckshot, on that day, I would've pummeled Mr. Porter with what I knew about my mother. I would've told him:

When Big Mama sent me to Jacksonville, North Carolina to live with my mother; my mother, then, sent me from Jacksonville, North Carolina to live with my father in Los Angeles, California; then my father sent me back from Los Angeles to Jacksonville, to live with my mother, her twos sons, and her live-in boyfriend Mr. Benny; after which my mother moved her two sons, Mr. Benny and myself to Augusta, Georgia. And finally, my mother sent me to live with my father in Richmond, California. My father left me in Richmond with my sixth grade best friend and went back to Los Angeles. As a result of his disappearance I turned myself over to the police. The police, as you can see, brought me here.

I wasn't in the mood to tell anymore than I had. Secretly. I was afraid that if I told them too much that I'd find myself back in Texas. Back with Lula Mae. When Mr. Porter completed the intake procedures he pushed a white button and spoke into the wall speaker. Within moments I walked down a long hallway behind a small Filipino woman, the color of an uncooked pinto bean. I carried a blanket, sheets and a toothbrush down a sterile, overly bright corridor. Electric-bright orange panic doors opened, and closed with the click of the metal air-handle, underneath a flickering exit sign.

My red Converse, the ones I'd stolen on a dare from K-Mart, screeched across the sterile linoleum floors announcing my arrival to the six unwanted teenaged girls already asleep within ear-shot of the counselor's bullpen. And a heavy-duty ring of keys jangled like sleigh bells from my escorts waistband every time she moved. I told myself anything would be better than Mrs. Bushfield.

Shortly thereafter, I, sat across the desk from Gail Maddy, the woman who'd led me to the Girls' section. The staff room with its white concrete walls, beige file cabinets and grey indoor-outdoor carpet was sparse except for the foot long, black tactical flashlight that lay on the desk next to a clipboard and a red leather-bound book titled: "Daily Record." Miss Maddy explained that I'd arrived during the graveyard shift. My mother, had worked those same shifts, and just hearing the words "graveyard shift" made me feel more at ease. "I see here that Mr. Porter asked you about your mother," she said looking straight into my eyes. "Is there anything you wish to tell me, about her?" Not sure of what to say, I turned my head quickly and stared out past the extra-thick safety glass surrounding the room, into the shadows of a darkened room just beyond where we sat.

Ms. Maddy explained that she'd be the one to stay in our section through the night. I imagined She'd keep watch over us until the sun towed daylight into the sky. Then, she'd hand over the giant loaded-down key ring to the a.m. relief staff and exchange details concerning the girls whose names were handwritten in the red book. Morning rounds would begin.

Love Had It's Own Smell

"Good morning, Pumpkin," said a perky white woman whose root beer colored hair moved about her shoulders in ropey whorls, the staff key ring jangled from her wrist. I sat up in the rickety bed. She had my attention. In between the spaces she moved, from bed-to-floor-floor-to-bed, shaking this one's toes, picking up discarded blankets restoring them neatly at the foot of that one's bed, shaking that one's toe. "My name ain't no Punkin," I said, rolling my eyes, swiveling my neck, two moves all little black girls I knew had; our way of establishing ground, letting whoever it was know we weren't to be trifled with. "I know," the white woman said, and placed her hands upon the tops of my knees. I cringed. Big Mama had long ago warned me that white people were the only folks she'd known who could "go bare-footed with hot pants on in the dead of winter without catching they death in sickness." She'd told me to stay clear of 'em, unless, of course, I wanted their ways to rub off onto me." This woman smiled generously, and spoke to me in ways I hadn't been on the receiving end of. Although the new situation was unnerving in that I didn't know what I'd gotten myself into, I felt a tightening loosen, in my gut. "Your name is Regina. Welcome to the shelter." "What's your name," I asked.

Cream of Wheat, warmed Pet Milk, vanilla with a bit of brown sugar—that's what the smell brought to my mind when Miss Kerr crouched down to meet my gaze. Her breath reached across the small space between the two of us. Pulling me in. The scent fixed itself upon me and clung to my skin in a veil as thin as a baby's breath, staining me the way odor does a baby bird when a human hand touches it. Like the bird, I was marked forever: Love had its own smell.

"Please, come with me." I slid off the bed and followed her lead. We bypassed the small staff room I'd sat in the night before, and walked against a crowd of kids—no older than I was—who seemed anxious to get outdoors. They slammed through the panic doors, and assaulted the air with swear words, and arm farts, as their angry feet stomped down hard against the cracked, brittle earth. The straggly ways they were dressed, the jitteriness in their eyes mixed with the smell left in their wake reeked of being unwanted.

In another room, called the nurses' station, Miss. Kerr studied a series of "X's" on the outline drawing of a body. The whole thing felt like we were on one of those television detective shows.

Miss Kerr turned the form towards me, pointed to the nearest "X" on my forehead. "Who did this to you?" I sat quietly. Miss Kerr waited patiently.

Mrs. Bushfield got away scot-free.

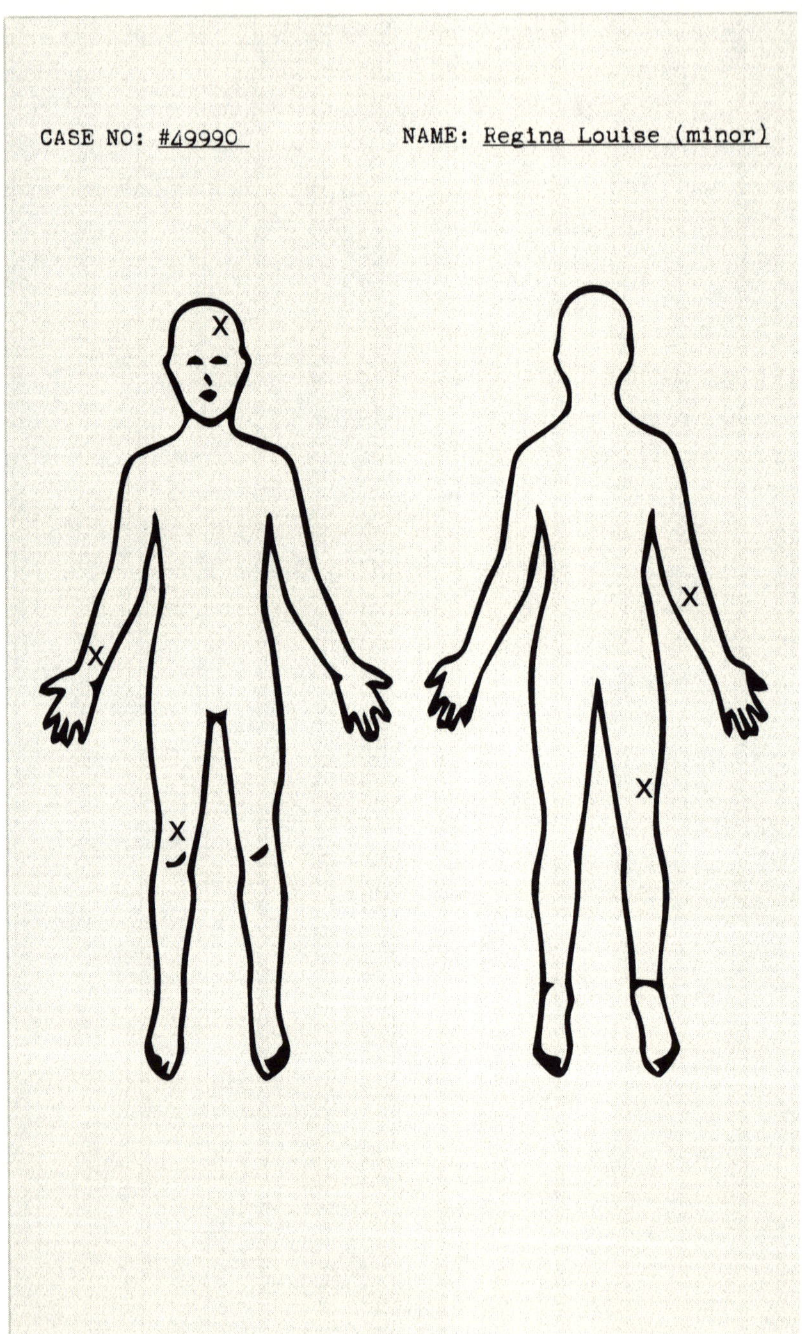
CASE NO: #49990

NAME: Regina Louise (minor)

After Miss Kerr and I finished in the nurse's station, she escorted me back to the staff's office. I went back to the bedroom and grabbed my personal belongings.

I handed over:

1) the clothes off my back
2) a half-smoked Kool long cigarette from my pocket along with
3) a mood ring and
4) the baggie with the toilet paper, in exchange for a pair of shorts and a shirt.

Ten ways to best use toilet paper is to:

Blow your nose into it

Wrap it around your hand till the wad is thick enough to use a menstruation napkin

Stuff it into your bra to prevent you from looking like a tomboy

Make shoes that are too-big-for-you fit

Tear it, then twist it into pieces and use as a roller

Pretend you have the Kentucky-Fried chicken man's moustache

Spit nasty food into it: Peas. Okra. Cod Liver Oil. Ambrosia Fruit Cake. Flush it

Hock a loogie into

Wipe your behind.

Wipe snuff-juice from around Big Mama's lips.

Dry your face before you really get something to cry for.

✓ Hold the last kiss my mother was ever going to give me.

Make A Wish

Inside of Swanson's Ice Cream Parlor the tables were filled with high-pitched voices, kids ran freely, wildly through the room. And no one seemed to mind. The adults did not slap the kids as a reminder of how rotten they were, there was no one chastising them about how they were going to burn in hell for causing "too much racket." Families huddled together around tables inside red leather booths that resembled half-eaten sour cherry balls, and music poured from the on-the-table-juke boxes. Electricity filled the air and somehow matched what I felt like on the inside, most of the time. Excited, I suddenly had an idea of what it meant to be happy. The scene reminded me of what family looked like, sounded like and felt like at my friend Mary's house. These strangers, and my friend Mary's family had made it look so easy, being kind. Why couldn't my own family be like that?

Poverty was a robber baron.

Helium-filled balloons hung from the ceiling by colorful ribbons, and I wanted to grab them all. I wanted to grab them all and run my way through California, Arizona and the top of New Mexico until I reached South Austin, until I reach 2524 South Fifth Street, where I'd find Lula Mae sitting there, in front of her black and white television with the aluminum foiled rabbit ears, and the vice grip pliers used as the rotary dial to change the channels. I'd interrupt her stupid "stories" and shove those balloons into her face and say, "See, I'm gonna be somebody."

Miss Kerr walked towards a table that sat in the middle of the room. The workers in their white short-sleeve red striped shirts with bow ties, khakis and silly hats reminded me of Burt from Mary Poppins. Three guys sang happy birthday to a boy. He swung his little head from side to side, and licked his tongue out at the folks gathered around him, they laughed, pointed, snapped a Polaroid. He was not accused of being ungrateful. Stupid. It's as if they expected him to act that way, and it was okay to do so. The folks I came from would never have tolerated that. That may've been one of the first times I witnessed—up front—the differences between how whites and blacks interacted with their children. The differences in expectations.

It was an incredibly impressionable time for me. And without knowing the socio-racial implications of what it meant to be displaced, black, and female, all I wanted was to be wanted, celebrated, and accepted for the gutsy girl I was. I needed to hear that I was okay blossoming into my own even if I was doing it while simultaneously bumping up against the limitations of a color-struck society. So what.

Before I ever had a chance to protest, a gaggle of workers made their way through the parlor, towards our table carrying a white cake, sprinkled around the sides with every color in the rainbow. They stopped in front of our table. The guy holding the cake sat it down, and it read *Happy Birthday, Regina*, in pink icing and all I could allow myself to do was laugh. I was speechless. Another someone offered me balloons, and yet another, blew into a bazooka to establish pitch. They sang me happy birthday, and without realizing it, I'd scooted in closer to Miss Kerr. I'd never before heard, that I was "shy." It felt good knowing what shy felt like. It felt good to pull back, not have to be the one in charge of me.

"Close your eyes and make a wish," Miss Kerr directed. I closed them, and Miss Kerr placed the arm closest to me around me and pulled me close. It was warm, her kind of joy. She made love look easy, feel easy.

I sank into her embrace, and somewhere in the holding on, I made a wish to never have to let go.

Not so unlike falling in love with a boy, or a boy with a girl (with the exception of a kiss): I fell in love with Jeanne Kerr shortly after the trip to the ice cream parlor; shortly after we got back to the shelter and those kids who got to go home on the weekends to be with their own families: Tammy, Valencia, Trudy and Dana, argued to stay behind and hang with the "nice white lady."

They wanted some of what she was giving to me, they wanted to be seen and heard and called names that lifted their lives up from the lowest common denominators of poverty, loss and being unwanted, I could sense it from the glimmer in their eyes that they wanted to feel what it was like to have their lives spinning around, and around, moving up and down like they were their very own carousel ride: I was destined to be a swan.

Any time I had the chance, I was happy to have Miss Kerr all to myself. No one from my bloodline, or otherwise came to visit, called, or wrote me love letters about how they missed me so much, and just couldn't wait to set eyes upon me, once again. They put no hands around my slender shoulders and pulled me close. They didn't seem that concerned with never letting me go. Every day I felt my family slipping away, leaving, and there was nothing I could about it.

Weekend Leftovers

Tom lived a thirty-minute-drive away from Martinez & ECS, but somehow managed to concoct a world of his own where I did not exist, a worldview whereas he suddenly put his paternity into question. Clearly love had nothing to do with how he felt about me. I gave that man every chance in the world to respond to me, by calling him, writing him and sending messages between him and my then social worker Alma Martin.

Although highly inappropriate, I spent an entire day, once, crocheting my father a condom.* I wrapped the covering, tied a bow around it, and sent it to him via Ms. Martin. In all honesty, I never stopped to try and understand how "concerning" that was, to give my own father such a gift. The Christmas before he'd given me a jar of pickled pig's feet. I thought he was attempting to be funny. If not his, whose job was it to model for me what was good and earnest? Whose job was it to set appropriate boundaries and hold to them as if he were active military frontline personnel who'd give his own life to keep me safe at night? I guess I never saw Tom the way a *real* daughter might. He wasn't able to see me the way a father might. We just didn't have it like that. Also, growing

---

*I decided that he clearly didn't need anymore children.

up in an institution had its limits. I was at an age where I was not only beginning to understand my own sexuality, but also I lived in an extremely repressive environment where those things—of a sexual nature—were simply not discussed.

Tom never personally responded to the gift, the happy birthday card Miss Kerr helped me put together for him (she hadn't known about the gift.) I heard from my social worker Tom thought I needed help, that I needed the Lord more so then than ever. Tom never said, "I love you." I rejected what felt like his indifference to my being alive. I began to reject him as he rejected me.

So, instead, I fell deeper in love with the way Miss Kerr called me "Sweetheart" when we weren't at the shelter, maybe driving down the street on our way to an outing like swimming at the YMCA in Pleasant Hill, or a 7-Eleven store run. The way she said it, "Sweetheart," made my heart feel like a sun with a thousands rays reaching out to touch every part of life, like anything I could think to do was actually possible simply because I'd been called, and seen as a sweetheart.

I was head-over heels when, as a result of my running away to get to her house before her shift at ECS ended, I was allowed to sleepover at Miss Kerr's. It was close to 9:00 p.m. when I sneaked from my bed, shoes in hand.

I tiptoed past the staff office and headed for the side door next to the *Girls'* bathroom. I quietly pushed on the panic door exit handle and once outside, quickly put on my Converse, and jumped the fence that surrounded the facility.

Earlier that day, Ms. Kerr had taken a few of us girls, who were the "weekend leftovers" on a joy ride. Along the way we had to stop at her apartment 140 Flora Avenue. I made it a point to imprint her address onto my brain by repeating it over and over again and by the time I set out to find my way back to her house it was as if I already knew my way home. "What are you doing here?" Miss Kerr asked, as surprised to see me there as I was for her to ask me *why* I was there. In my mind, when she'd brought me over it was cool. My inviting myself felt just as cool. Miss Kerr called the overnight staff at ECS and explained where I was, and that she'd be happy to bring me back the next day.

She gave me my very own toothbrush and squeezed toothpaste onto it. I took my time to brush. I wanted that moment to last forever. Miss Kerr handed me a long white night gown that had what seemed like a hundred buttons down the front and I felt like Louisa May Walcott, or one of the Walton's girls. I half expected to hear Miss Kerr call out "Goodnight, John Boy," right before she quietly said: "Goodnight, sweetheart, sleep tight."

Anything

"You can be anything you want, sweetheart," Miss Kerr told me one day while helping me pack my belongings into a *Glad garbage* bag. It was Ms. Martin's last attempt to place me in a foster home, and she'd hoped that like a much-needed kidney transplant, I'd take. Take to the family like white on rice, hand to glove, skin to flesh, like nobody's business, like a starving fool, like a fish to water,

Like hells to the no: I had other plans.

Miss Kerr was a dream-making Apostle who proselytized about making one's dreams come true; her words baptized me into thinking that I could be whatever I wanted to. Her words baptized me into becoming a believer. I believed.

IF I wanted to I could be...

1. Famous
2. a ballet dancer
3. a singer
4. a beautician
5. a model
6. a counselor like Miss kerr
7. a famous mother to ten children

I Got Glad

By the time Ms. Martin's white county car with the gold emblazoned stickers of the State of California plastered on both the drivers' and passenger's side doors peeled out of the driveway of the random house she'd dropped me off at, belonging to some random family, in a random part of the East Bay: I'd already said my pleasantries to both the wife and the husband, and scoped out my escape route: the window of the random bedroom I'd be expected to learn to live with, and slipped five dollars from the women's pocket book for bus fare.

The room had one bunk bed, and a twin. None of the sheet sets, or quilts, or blankets matched: checkered fitted sheets were nappy to the touch, and the checks collided with faded flowered sheets that reminded me of a pattern that could only be found on the top a jigsaw puzzle box.

The whole thing smacked of old people needing kids for the money. I became dizzy with not wanting to stay in that house another minute. Nothing matched my sensibility of how I wanted to feel. That house, and its rooms, and beds were nothing like Miss Kerr's house with her soft sheet sets, that comforter filled with down feathers she'd called a "duvet." It sounded fancy, royal. *You can be anything you want, sweetheart* I wanted to be wrapped in fancy. *You can be anything you want, sweetheart.*

I wanted to be back with Miss Kerr. I walked back to the shelter.

300 VS. 602

Are you a three hundred, or a six-o-two?" The light-skinned girl with the pinky-length pigtails asked. Her name was Valencia. She had a pinched nose that turned up slightly at the tip, and the hair that circled her face like duck down was held down with Vaseline in s-curves and flattened-out curlicues. She set the trend way before for Michael Jackson had. She was cool. "I don't know?" I told her. "You don't know? She came back, her chagrin for my stupidity sprung all over her face. "Ain't that what I just said? I asked wondering why all of a sudden the girl wanted to talk to me. Other than hanging out with Miss Kerr, I hadn't made many friends at the shelter. Kids came and went quicker than I could learn their names. "Ain't that about a B?" she said, "I know you ain't try to get smart with me, road kill?" "My name ain't road kill," I said. "It may not be now, but if you keep on getting' smart it will be," she called herself threatening me. I laughed. Hard. She laughed. Harder. We both fell out laughing. Hard. Together.

From that moment on, Valencia became my first friend at ECS. She was a street kid from North Richmond who was ever truant and flat-out refused to step foot onto the schools' grounds let alone walk into a classroom. She peddled uppers for her brother on the side but was busted for ditching school. I too, was truant, off and on, but for different reasons. I loved school and the only thing that kept me from it; the learning, the teachers, the reading, the writing, madrigal choir and art, was my continuous need to have a place to stay.

I let V, as I came to call her, school me on the differences between a 300 and a 602.

Ways To Become A 300

1. Three hundred is when you done had your ■ whipped and they left marks
2. Left behind in an abandoned building for days on end with no running water
3. Your mama takes off with a man promising to return soon as she can, and she never returned
4. Daddy goes to jail
5. When your blood won't take you in

Ways To Become A 602

1. At the top of your lungs you threaten to bust the car windows out of your boyfriend's car after you caught him with another girl, and someone called the police for you disturbing the peace
2. Peeing on the lawn of the one who reported you to police for threatening your boyfriend
3. Following through on the threat and busting windows out of your boyfriend's car

I was a three hundred. A Ward of the Court. So was V. Her boyfriend refused to press charges. She was lucky. She got off with a warning.

Black

"You are black, you know, Regina?

Six months had rolled around by the time I'd ran off six different caseworkers and met the woman who would become my social worker for the duration of my status as a ward of the court. We sat, Gwen Forde and I, in a small visiting room adjacent to the office where intakes took place. Ms. Forde was a petite coffee colored woman who wore twin sets, (the outer sweater always draped around her shoulders made her look like a caped crusader), A-line skirts and kitten heels. Two strings of glossy pearls looped around her neck. A moisture heavy mole sat perched above her upper lip, and it moved when she spoke. Her mole was a spy.

Gwen Forde's Afro was cut close, military regulation tight, and if I didn't see her face-to-face, If I hadn't been right there, in the room with her, if I hadn't seen her with my very own eyes, watched her tongue move rapidly around in her mouth about my being "black," I would have sworn with my life that Gwen Forde, her speech practiced, each vowel articulated with precision was as white as any white person I'd met. I couldn't see how what she accused me of being was any different from how she showed up. I wished I could've understood better, the politics of codified language.

A Superior Judge from the Juvenile court division had appointed Gwen Forde to my case. Gwen Forde's job was to make sure that

I got what I needed: somewhere to live, a decent family that would accept me, take me in as their own. A black family. They must be "black" Gwen Forde, insisted as though I were fighting her on the matter. Black. "The family will most likely be black, like you," she said.

Whenever Gwen Forde spoke to me it was hard for me to listen, hard for me to stay right where I was. When Gwen Forde spoke my mind took leave from the room, the passengers side of the car, the courtroom, the lunchroom, the counselors office, visiting office. After the first sentence was uttered from her mouth I was off and running. Searching. Confused. Sometimes I wondered if people picked on us kids because we were easy targets.

I wondered if they were aware that they could do or say almost anything and get away with it, if they wanted to. After all, who was there to believe us, over them. I wondered if Gwen was mad as heck because she thought I was getting something she couldn't or didn't want from white people. Maybe she didn't want me to want anything from a white person. Or maybe it was white people she was really mad at, and not me. I always wondered. "Why do you always have to start with my being black?" I asked her one day. "What is that about?" I had to know.

Gwen told me it was about *me*. She swore that I was not black enough, didn't know what it meant to be black and that I acted as if being black was too good for me. I didn't understand her. There was no time to follow the movement and keep myself abreast of what was happening on the front of black politics. I would not have known where to get started. Everything around me was white; the counselors, the county cars, the therapists, the judges, the teachers, and volunteers. Television. Radio.

I didn't give a care to what was going on in the world beyond the most basic and primitive need: I wanted my mother or somebody who could want me the way she was supposed to. Didn't Gwen know: Trauma was colorless? Attachment was primal. "You're manipulative, Regina. You've run from so many homes I'm afraid they'll be nowhere else to place you. I didn't know what "manipulative" meant. I didn't know what most of the words Gwen used to describe me meant. Anyhow, what did that have to do with my being black?

I wouldn't know about Martin Luther King, Shirley Chisholm or Rosa Parks until three years later when I'd attend a public high school for the first time, at seventeen and a half.

Flight Risk

During the time I spent at Edgar Children's Shelter, I failed more than twenty-seven trial runs to potential foster families in the San Francisco Bay Area. One county vehicle after another dropped me off in:

Pittsburgh
Antioch
Stockton
Martinez
Sacramento
Richmond
San Francisco
Martinez
El Cerrito
Oakland
Martinez
Redding
Concord
Richmond
San Francisco
Pittsburgh
Martinez
Antioch

Richmond
San Francisco
Martinez
San Francisco
Martinez
Stockton
Martinez
El Cerrito
North Richmond
Stockton
San Francisco.

Oakland
Concord
Martinez
Redding
Stockton
Oakland
Francisco
Sacramento
San Francisco
Concord
Redding
Oakland
Concord
Stockton
Oakland
North
Martinez
El

Each time, I stepped out of a white county vehicle carrying my personal belongings in either a *Glad* garbage bag or a brown paper sack. There was no room for shame in what I carried.

Those twenty-seven times my placements "failed to take," sometimes it was because the men in those homes wanted to have their way with me; especially the home where the Preacher lived with his son and two daughters. Years later, while watching a television news program I learned that the allegations of neglect and abuse were filed against that same family.

Gwen Forde also knew, before the news broke.

I went as far as to try and tell Gwen Forde—exactly—how the Preacher's son *really* was. I tried to tell her how he thought of himself as a "Pimp in the Pulpit." I told Gwen Forde how he peeped at me while I undressed, through a small hole he'd drilled into the bathroom door. And how I stuck a Q-tip into the hole. He blamed the destruction of the property on me. An incident report was filed against me.

And then, there was the time he walked by me, while I was getting my hair pressed by one of the other girl's in the house, and he leaned over and whispered in my ear how he'd rape me if I opened my big mouth about our little secrets. Gwen Forde said that I was jealous that my hair was nappy, and not long and wavy and good, like the Preacher's daughters'. I tried to tell Gwen Forde about how the Preacher's son waited until the household was asleep. How he'd open my bedroom door, slowly. How he'd spend what felt like hours to tiptoe towards my bed, pull the sheet back, and how the sound of his zipper-drowned out my heartbeats.

How he led himself, in hand, between my sixteen year-old thighs and tried to force himself into me.

How I pretended to be asleep, and fought him off at the same time thinking he'd think it was all a dream and make it end.

How his breath hummed of doo-doo and collard greens. The way he threatened to "bust my █████" just for fun if, I ever told.

How he said that I was the reason my mama and daddy hated me, wished they'd never had me, and looked forward to the day I died.

I told Gwen Forde what he said: "You ain't the first piece of foster girl ███ I ever had. You bastard girls, ya'll all the same. Don't nobody gives a damn about y'all." I told Gwen Forde how he visited my bedroom off and on for the next six months. I told her that I wanted to leave. She accused me of "making things up again." She said that I was a natural born "storyteller," with an "incredible" knack for exaggeration. She said that there was no other place for me to go, that my reputation "preceded me." I didn't understand. She said that unlike the little white girls that came and went so quickly, I wasn't fortunate like them to have daddies to write checks to finance their craziness. She said that feeling bad about my life was a luxury I couldn't afford. She said that what I needed was a black family, or at least "two strong black women," women who would see through my "cutesy girl" antics. She said that white people were gullible and that's the only reason Miss Kerr liked me. She felt sorry for me, that she got to act out her savior complex on me. She said that I thought I was white. She said that I was suffering from an identity crisis.

I asked Gwen if she'd want to take someone like me home with her given how black her own skin was.

I asked Gwen if it would be okay if I lived with Miss Kerr?

She threatened to place me in Napa State Hospital, in the "children's psyche ward."

I saw no other choice but to run from that home too.

What Do You See

Early December. 1977. The white county car skulked around the hills of El Cerrito, California and I learned to call the passenger seat shotgun. Parked alongside a curb, Gwen Forde spun the steering wheel until the wheels pointed towards the good doctor's front door. It was painted red. Once inside, I took the seat offered to me by a woman I imagined was the good doctor's secretary and while she was pretty with her long Cindy Brady hair she wasn't prettier than Miss. Kerr.

The not prettier than Miss Kerr secretary led me into another room. Behind a great big dark wood desk sat Dr. Cohen. He sat in a swivel chair. Behind him, on a long narrow table were photos of what I imagined to be a younger version of him with a woman, a boy and two girls. The smaller girl held onto a ginger-red dog, an Irish Setter named "Daisy," Dr. Cohen said when I stared at the photo probably longer than I should have. It was the closest I'd been to a dog real or otherwise.

Dr. Cohen stood, reached for my hand and upon contact our hands wilted; I wasn't sure who was afraid to touch whom. He got right to it, Dr. Cohen did. He picked up a large deck of cards and explained that all I needed to do was tell him what I saw in each card he held up. I was immediately insulted. I felt as if my whole being were being challenged, as if there was something wrong with me that I didn't know about and that the doctor was trying to get at on the sly.

I sucked my teeth, and turned away at the first photo. I became increasingly impatient. "Take your time," the doctor said and I sat there, chewed my fingernails, and rocked one leg up and down. "Tell me," the good doctor said, "tell me, Regina, exactly what you believe you see in this picture I am holding up for you."

I saw a lot of images in the card he held up: a mean looking cat, a possessed pumpkin head, a pissed-off Wile E. Coyote. I saw how stupid it was for a grown man to pour ink onto paper, fold it in half, like a slow kindergartener, and then have the nerve to ask me what the ████ it was. If he didn't know, how was I supposed to know? He continued to hold that ██████ card up until I gave him something he could hold onto, until I gave him reason to lift up his fancy pen and write down on that white note pad he'd scribble on in between holding up those childish cards. We waited one another out.

Finally, I decided I was done messing with that stupid game so I gave him what I thought he wanted: "I see two of them little bitty Mexican dogs fighting over a roasted marshmallow on a stick." "No, wait," I said. "I see two of them little bitty Mexican dogs trying to hold on tight, with all of their might to a pogo stick."

A couple of days prior to my appointment with Dr. Cohen, the staff at ECS had taken the girls' section on an all-day outing where we'd ended the evening by each of us having to collect a stick to toast a marshmallow over a fire in order to make s'mores. We also took turns learning to bounce up and down on a pogo stick. Made sense to me.

Pressed Chinos And A Shirt That Matched

It was June, of 1978. I was finally having my semi-annual dependency hearing, during which Gwen Forde and a judge decided whether or not I was fit for a family setting, or should be placed in a residential treatment facility. Gwen presented the case of my "inability to stay put."

The courtroom was small, but larger than Andy Griffith's. The walls, marbled black and white, were cold to the touch. I sat catty-cornered to the flagpole left of the judge's bench. My back against the wall. My case, the only one on the docket that day.

"All rise," said a large man dressed in dark chinos and a shirt that matched. The bailiff called out: "This is a dependency hearing for minor: REGINA OLLISON case#49990-(16)-Born: May 2, 1962, Austin Texas. Who represents the minor?" My social worker rose from her chair raised her hand and swore on the Bible to "Tell the truth, the whole truth and nothing but the truth."

"Your honor," Gwen proceeded, "For all intents and purposes, both of minor's parents have relinquished custody." No one had told me as much.

I sat quietly, and waited. I hoped I'd get a turn to tell the truth, the whole truth, and nothing but the truth about what I wanted.

"Be brave, sweetheart," Miss Kerr had told me that morning. Miss Kerr had gone as far as to say that perhaps one day we could live together. She'd asked me how I felt about that. She'd read my mind, said what I couldn't. By then, I'd not heard one word from either of my parents. I hardly ever thought of Big Mama, or my sister. The idea of Miss Kerr rejecting me was too much. But I was glad she had the guts to ask. "You think Gwen would ever let that happen?" I asked, unable to hold a conversation about the question she'd asked me, afraid that somehow something bad might happen if I let myself believe that I deserved the good she offered, let myself speak it out loud as if it was already done. Miss Kerr didn't respond.

Miss Kerr promised to take me to Hawaii, to have us live amongst her relatives who lived there. She was born of royal Hawaiian descendants and said they'd accept me as their own. She wanted me to feel comfortable in my skin, be around others who were my same color.

Secretly, from that moment on I tried to piece together the scenes of what it would be like to live with Miss. Kerr. I saw myself in an "outside" school, where I'd get to raise my hand in hopes of being called on because I'd studied hard the night before. I'd become the teacher's pet and get to leave class whenever I wanted. I'd become trustworthy. Miss. Kerr would not only watch me, but question and cross examine what I'd learned until we were both satisfied I had the right answer. I saw myself peeling the crumpled dollar bill and fifty cents that she'd given me for my lunch out of the front pocket of my jeans, and hand it to the lunch cashier. I'd dodge the shame that came along with a free-lunch ticket.

I'd learn to look forward to my birthday and over time acquire a taste for my favorite cake, and not only have the courage to ask for it, but also, maybe I'd learn to make friends again, like

Sandra Perez, back in South Austin. Maybe I could have my own party, in my own house and invite my own friends, sleep in my own room. And more than that, I saw myself, at the end of a long day, standing curbside, backpack heavy with homework, broken pencils, and crumbs from the cookies she would've sent with me, and picture-day forms requiring my parent's immediate attention. There I'd be waiting for Miss Kerr to swerve around the corner in her blue Oldsmobile. She'd named it the Blue Swan. And just when I thought she'd perhaps changed her mind, and had decided to leave me there, because how could someone like her want me, she'd pull up. I'd get in. Off we would go, just like that, the two of us. "Will minor please approach the bench?"*4+9=13+9=22+9+0 is 31… 4+9=13+9=22+9+0 is 31…* Most of the words the bailiff spoke held no meaning for me. Except, that is, for the five numbers that identified my case from all the other children in foster care. *4+9=13+9=22+9+0 is 31…* In an effort to calm my nerves, to allow the story of Miss Kerr and I to come through, I added the numbers that identified my case together: *4+9=13+9=22+9+0 is 31…* I let myself believe that in that moment, there was no number in the world more powerful than the number 31. All I would have to do is chant it repeatedly—*4+9 =13+9=22+9+0 is 31*—and somehow a magical power would be released to me. I would use it as I pleased. Couldn't everyone in that courtroom see that the number 31 turned around became 13? That was the day I'd met Miss Kerr. She'd been the one to say, "Look, today is your birthday." I didn't know my birthday from any other day. "Is there anything you'd like to say on your behalf, young lady?"

The judge spoke from behind a tan colored desk. A podium, and a long-necked microphone separated us. "I want to live with Miss. Kerr." I said. The judge shuffled through some papers, glanced over at Gwen Forde. "Counselor, who is Miss Kerr? The Judge asked Gwen. "Your Honor, may I approach the bench?" Gwen asked. She walked over to the judge and handed him papers in a file. Silence. "I am to understand that this Miss Kerr is a counselor at the Edgar Children's Shelter, where you are currently being detained?" "Yeah." "Okay, thank you," the judge said, closing the file. "Bailiff, at this time, will you please escort minor from the courtroom." The Bailiff slanted his hand beside me and led me from the podium, down the short aisle, into the courthouse hallway. I sat on a bench outside the courtroom doors and waited for Gwen.

Shortly thereafter the judge made his decision.

Started To Stand Naked

I'd arrived at Guideways just as the trees started to stand naked against the backdrop of a late September sky, and I was nearly sixteen and a half.

Guideways was a level-fourteen residential treatment center fully staffed to handle the emotionally charged disturbances of adolescent girls. The staff at Guideways was going to rehabilitate my behavior. They were a 24/7 facility with the ability to provide psychotropic medication support. It was supposed to be "A 'last-ditch' effort" before I was again, threatened to be shipped off to the Napa State Hospital adolescent ward.

I'd heard they had a wing for children just like me at Napa State, children who were so far beyond the reach of psychological interventions like talk-therapy, and behavior modification programs. The joke was: kids like me forced anyone who'd come into contact with us to become emotionally taxed, exhausted, we weren't worth the effort it would take to save us. That's what staff said.

Gwen Forde pulled her white county car into the slot marked "Visitor" and ordered me out of the car. Gwen Forde popped all four-door locks at once setting my heart racing. I was a sprinter stuck in my running block, going nowhere fast.

I wished her luck getting me to move.

I Thought About

I sat in that white county car and thought back to the last time I saw Miss Kerr. I thought about how I ran to the girls' section, needing to find her, about how I'd heard someone yell at me to "stop running," but their words fell flat behind me. I thought about how I rounded the corner, and heard someone crying. Hard. It was a grown-woman-kind-of-crying, not a girls. I thought about how I crossed the doorway leading from the long hall that separated the boys' section from the girls', the main office from the living quarters, into the dining area. About how I'd found Miss Kerr, lying on the kitchen floor, her legs drawn up close to her as though she were a small child. She yowled. I thought about the seconds it took for me to get across the room, how I kneeled down beside her; how when I'd asked her what the matter was she'd said:

"I...tried...to make you...my daughter, today."

When

"You're just plain hateful, Regina," Gwen said, and pulled the key from the ignition. That's not what I needed to hear from Gwen. I needed to know when I'd get to see Miss Kerr again. "Why don't you ask me what I want?" I asked Gwen. I was no longer afraid of Gwen. Once I realized she didn't *really* like me, that she didn't *really* want what was best for me, that she couldn't put her hands on me, I also realized I could say just about anything I wanted to. I had a say. "C'mon and do it!" I screamed. "Do it! Ask me what I want?" I let the rage settle in between us. I gave Gwen all the time I could to say what was on her mind. "Ask me: What do you want, Regina?" "Fine. I'll ask myself," I decided. Gwen already thought I was crazy. "What do you want Regina?" I asked out loud. "What do *you* want Regina?"

"I want to walk down the street with Miss Kerr. I want to reach for her hand to thread my fingers through hers, and to swing our arms back and forth, up and over, back and forth, up and over churning forever down, down into our bones. I want to be like any other girl. Maybe I want to know what it might feel like to call Miss Kerr: 'Mama.'"

A Whole Lot Of "If's"

"Bravo!" Gwen said clapping. "If that's what you want, Regina, then you'll need to show me something a lot more interesting than that crazy-show you just put on. You can fool the psychiatrist, your white lady friend, but you don't fool me." Gwen stepped out of the car, grabbed her brief case, and slammed the door. Walked around to my side. I sat there. I was worn out from the heat, the almost three-hour drive with traffic, and the heaviness of yet another blow-up with Gwen, another placement; more girls to get to know; more stories about their messed-up families, more eyes to echo back to me what I didn't have, and what I probably wasn't ever going to have according to Gwen, more staff members, doctors, rules, ways I needed to act.

"If you don't want me to write up an incident report of verbal assault, I suggest you start rethinking how to speak to me," Gwen threatened as she yanked the passenger door open. "Get out of my car, now! I'd never seen Gwen so hyped–up.

"And another thing: If you don't get out, I will call back-up and make it so that you don't see the inside of another car for the rest of your time in care." Uncertain whether or not she could make that happen: I stepped out of the car. Gwen popped the trunk. I grabbed hold of my garbage bag and started towards the building.

Just as we stepped up to the front door of Guideways, Gwen turned, and said in a voice I had to strain in order to make out what she was saying: "If you ever want to see your precious Miss Kerr again, I suggest you make this placement stick like vanilla to ice cream. That is your favorite flavor, right, vanilla?"

I never came to understand the digs that Gwen seemed so inclined to make at my expense. I couldn't name—specifically—the feeling that came over me whenever I was around her, but she seemed hell bent on pushing me towards the edge of having a distaste for my own skin color. I felt like I wasn't okay being just who I was. That there was a secret way to being black—her particular kind of black—and she was down right aggravated that I didn't know the rules, so as punishment for my ignorance she made it clear that I wasn't good enough to join her club. I was a child, not her equal.

Gwen had every opportunity to educate me the way she wanted, if that's what she wanted. She could've given me books to get me up to speed on what it meant to be black—her kind of black. She could've told me stories about her family and the ways they did things. It could've been a way to supplement, or keep me in the know of what was happening in black folks' lives. She could've told me about the politics of the Black Panthers, the importance of Black Power and the struggle these movements intended to elucidate; the importance of why it was necessary for me to connect my sense of individual identity to that of a national identity as well. She could've sent newspaper clippings, sent book club subscriptions.

Back then, I may not have known what her big words meant, or understood the revulsion beneath the cock-eyed looks she'd give, but the feeling I had when I left her, more often than not, left me wondering: if I were found at the site of a train wreck, and Gwen were to come and identify my body, I imagined she'd see me lying there, all broken up, trapped, unable to move. She'd lock eyes with mine, make sure that I saw her, stick her hands in her coat pocket, and walk right on past me with a snigger that satisfied her all the way home.

I am grateful for time, it's gift of allowing my feelings and attitude to soften into a better sense of understanding. Compassion.

It Did Not Matter

We weren't supposed to: touch one another, or sit so close that body contact became an arguable matter; borrow anyone's personal belongings; socks, underwear, tooth brushes, clothing items, hair brushes, shampoo, *Summer's Eve*, or another residents prescribed medications; we weren't to instigate an already escalating situation on it's way to becoming an incident; we were to keep or comments to ourselves, our mouths shut; we weren't encouraged to express emotional frustration in the television room or any other room where residents were likely to gather; the van, the swimming pool area, the kitchen or at the dining room table; we were not to receive mail, care packages, love letters, letters of concern from a family member, a friend, an ex-counselor, previous staff we may've had a relationship with prior to our residency at Guideways who had not been re-vetted then placed on our "call lists"; it did not matter if your social worker knew the person (s) before we arrived; it did not matter if said person already had established evidence of a positive connection; we weren't to leave the grounds without a staff escort; attend any outside activities, schools, social excursions, occasions or anything that would require a judge's decision; we weren't to apply for after school jobs, local community center theatre productions, paper routes; we would need to earn our way onto "Level one" and keep it for the duration of one month before earning the privilege to smoke; to call one person who'd been approved; to go for joy rides in van with staff to the local 7-Eleven; we would need to earn "Level two" in order to go to the mall with a purchase order to *Sears & Roebuck* or *J.C. Penney's* with a staff member in tow; we would need to earn "Level three" to have our own room, a full closet, shared bath and the right to have other residents visit your room; we weren't allowed to have sex on, or off the property; no alcohol or contraband items included, marijuana, hash, cocaine, heroine or pipes; we could not attend outside schools without a judge's decree. We lived in the landscape of could not, weren't allowed to, weren't supposed to.

In Every Manner Of The Word

On a blisteringly hot Saturday night, a solid month of successfully abiding by the Guideways' rules beneath my belt, I sat in Lolita's room on the edge of her bed my eyes closed as she drew cool water into the small bathtub at the opposite end of the room. She was one of the residents who'd played by the rules and earned the gold level—level three—faster than anyone ever had which meant she'd scored her own room, own schedule, relationships with staff who seemed to bend to her will, her own way of doing things.

It was her choice that I come and "hang out" in her room, just the two of us, while most of the other girls, along with the staff, were out for a night of roller-skating at the local rink. It was Lolita's night to wash her hair and she "sure as hell wasn't going to hang with any of them bunk girls who stayed drugged, lifeless and called attention to the fact that none of us were related." She'd seen me plait another resident's hair—a Mexican girl—and had commented on how quickly my fingers moved in and out of the dense curls.

I'd learned to plait hair in a dream. My sister, who braided with the quickness of a hummingbird, refused to teach me. So I'd watched her. I recorded each move she made at the speed she made it, and in my dreams I'd slow her fingers down and replace them with my own. When I awoke, I asked my sister if I could braid her hair, and did. I learned most everything like that.

Lolita's daddy had her move into her mother's side of the bed when her mama died. She became her daddy's second wife in every manner of the word *wife*. This grew her up fast, I imagined, and when that half-black, half Japanese girl, whose long black hair brushed the curve of her spine when she walked, lowered those eyes the shape of teardrops tilted towards Heaven, all I could do was whatever she told me to. I'd always had an inclination for the beauty of girls, their rituals. *

I was a tomboy. Rough. Rarely remembered to lotion my skin, change my underwear, wash my hair. Bathe. Always afraid I'd miss something I took as little time as possible with me. I needed to be in the mix, know what was going on, solving for not being left behind. I imagined there were things Lolita could show me if I were going to move through the behavior mod system at Guideways. I heard her slip into the water and I opened my eyes,

* They'd started with Sandra Rodriquez—rituals did—the girl back in South Austin. I'd wait till after school to fight kids. I'd jump them from behind a bush, garbage can, a tree. Sandra intervened, one day, when I targeted her friend. Sandra stood up to me and offered to become my friend if I spared her friend. I accepted. Over time, given I was sent home earlier than the other students to give me a head start to get home, and spare them a licking, Sandra agreed to leave the key to her house in a tear in her brother's motorcycle seat. The ritual: I'd go to her house, remove my clothes and hide. Sometimes I'd hide in a closet, beneath a bed. Sandra would arrive home; I'd listen while she searched for me, and whichever one of us found the other, first, got to do whatever she wanted. Sandra taught me how to touch her breasts, the outsides of our vagina's, named that feeling that comes with the touching: A pillow between us, we'd grind our narrow hips into one another as if we were one another's last breath. We kissed using our tongues. The game, "Hide-and-go-get-it" became one of my favorite pastimes. Sometimes I got into trouble just so that Sandra would chastise me. Gently. Afterwards, Sandra would clean herself up, remove any traces that I'd *been* there, that we'd been there.

and tried hard to not let them fall upon her nakedness for fear that somehow I'd see my own, and blush with secret embarrassment.

But, when Lolita said, "get on over here girl, and cool my back off," I thought not about refusing her, or what might happen if someone found out but more so, I thought of what it would feel like to touch another human being, a girl whose skin was four shades deeper than my own, which made her the *Reese's Peanut Butter Cup* dark outside to my peanut butter colored center and these things together reminded me of my sister who was the same color as Lolita, and someone I'd shared a bed with up until I left Texas five years prior, the two of us stuck together like stacked chairs. I yearned for a bit of both; the cupping, and my sister.

The penalty for an infraction of the rules; touching for instance, brought with it the loss of privileges and a possible level demotion depending on who it was, how many warnings had already been administered. If caught/found out, the accuser would backslide to the previous level, and after a few extra chores: sweeping, mopping and or a shift of Kitchen Patrol, the wrong-doer could earn the loss back by way of restored privileges. I'd earned level one, and still hadn't received permission to call Miss Kerr. I took the sponge Lolita offered.

My buttocks rested on the lip of the tub and I waited. Watched. Lolita twisted her hair into a chignon that sat upon her head crownlike. Lolita coroneted herself. With both hands I squeezed the heavy sponge and let the water run the length of her smooth skin again, and again. I scrubbed her back tenderly as if she were my own child, as if I loved her. I picked up the bar of *Ivory* soap, and painted her hair with it. My fingers buried deep I dug into her scalp, felt the shape of her head. Egg. For a minute, I was lost in the ritual, lost in the touching alone that seemed to save me, to help me remember once again what it felt like to be human, to be kind and useful, to be needed. I needed to be needed, to feel the weight of significance.

Loss

It was one thing to learn that Gwen wouldn't be attending my one-month review meeting that would acknowledge my success at Guideways and set me up for level II, and another to hear that she'd "lost one of her kids." I didn't know that Gwen was married. I couldn't imagine her having a boyfriend. A child out of wedlock? Never. I probed deeper, and asked Phyllis, the in-house social worker that'd delivered the news, why she thought Gwen had never let on that she had a kid, why she hadn't told me.

Gwen didn't have any kids of her own. I was correct: she was not married. Gwen had actually lost a boy, a client, fourteen, to a car accident. He'd stolen the car, drove too fast, the car got away from him. He crashed. DOA.

It was the first time, that time, I'd had a chance to imagine Gwen as human. I imagined what she must've felt like the instant she'd heard the news, her eyes suddenly moist with sorrow. I imagined that every now and again she'd had lunch with him, the deceased one, and maybe she was kind to him. I imagined she might be the only one who'd attend his funeral, send him off with a handful of flowers. Blue. Carnations. I sometimes wondered who would be there if anything ever happened to me. Who would they have called?

That day, the one where I learned about Gwen's loss, I also heard that given how well I'd done, attaining level I—and keeping it—

the staff thought it might be best if I try and maintain my status for another month. "It'll be a piece a cake for you," Phyllis said, nudged me with a knuckle. I asked if I could finally call Miss Kerr. I'd had to wait an entire month to make that call, to receive a call. I'd given them what they wanted. It was my turn.

She's Not Here

There was no dramatic outburst from me in the way of whooping and hollering. I did not curse at Phyllis or tell her that her teeth looked like tiny Chiclet's, which made it difficult to listen to anything she said because I was far too busy trying to count her teeth. I did not "blow up," as I watched Phyllis root through my file, pull out my call list and say: "She's not here. Jeanne Kerr is not on your approved call list."

There was no one on my call list except Gwen Forde.

S.c.h.e.h.e.r.a.z.a.d.e

School at Guideways residential was considered "on-grounds" although each day the residents packed into a brown and beige 1978 Econoline van and were driven to an abandoned elementary school site that had been reconstituted as a school for severely emotionally disturbed girls. Unlike typical schools with their halls that separated each classroom by grades, hallways lined with lockers, or gymnasiums where the educational community would gather together for assembly, our school was more like walking into the echo of desertion than a place to learn.

Guideways school had several modular buildings that were situated around an asphalt basketball court, a typical school-yard metal merry-go-round that was weathered and had to be started "Yabba-dabba-do" style. Someone would have to grab hold of one of the holding bars, get a running start either by pushing or pulling, and then jump on, lean into one of the holding stalls, and ride until either we became so dizzy we had to get off, or because the motion stopped, and somebody needed to start the whole push, pull, run, jump sequence all over again. Usually for me once was enough in order to realize it was fun, but too much heat, too much work.

A lone tetherball pole leaned out from a small pool of softened, and wrinkled asphalt. Redding could get up into the three digits easily. The entire site was surrounded by melting asphalt.

What I remembered about school, the routines that I looked forward to about as much as I looked forward to reading, P.E. and writing was: shopping for school supplies, and clothes. I loved the yellow Ticonderoga #2 pencils and how their leads could hold a point, the smell of the plastic see-thru pen and pencil holder with the top zipper, and *Scooby-Doo* and the gang smiling at me. They were things that were mine. The spiral notebooks and the way each page was cut and ruled perfectly on each side made me fall hard for paper. Many times I wrote far beyond the marginal lines. I always felt like I needed more room.

But the thing about being a ward, was that everything had to go through a process of approval. And it wasn't until a request from a resident was made known to a counselor, or a therapist that a purchase order was drafted, the amount agreed upon, signed, and then handed over to a social worker who'd send it off to the facility manager, who'd discuss its pending arrival to the resident each time she asked "How long is it gonna take?" Until finally—usually months later—in a meeting, the manager would inform the team that the requested P.O. had arrived and then there'd be a debate on who was going to take the resident who'd made the request to the mall. By then, at least for me, the thrill of starting school was gone.

I became motivated by the lessons-in-a-box series. These boxes were categorized by subjects; Math, Social Studies, History, Literature, Theatre. Once inside the classroom we'd take our seats, and after the teacher made a head-count we were expected to go to the box of the subject we'd left off from the day before. Mostly, my aim was to finish an entire grade level as quickly as I could in order to stay on track for college. Once, I'd discussed college as an option with Gwen and the look she gave me would've made ugly jealous. But it was already in my body, going to college was, and there was nothing Gwen could do to take that. I was already the somebody I knew I would one day be; I just needed time to find people who also believed. I needed time to come into myself, that was all. Time to come into my own.

My love for books had started when I was three or four years old. I don't remember the full chronology of how I developed the skill, but I do know that I read books, broke bread with books and on many a night I slept with my books, right there beneath my pillow where I'd place them, and sometimes inside the pillow case. It was Miss Kerr who'd told me to "Never skip over a world you don't know." I still had the dictionary/thesaurus she'd given me as a "going away" present. We never said 'goodbye.'

So, by the time I'd made it through the sixth, seventh, eighth, ninth and tenth grade boxes I'd read about the Constitution of the United States, had every word of "We the People…" memorized by heart, and understood the differences between "attained" and "ascribed" status enough to imagine that I could—one day—be more than what I was born into (ascribed), if I was willing to work for it (attained.) Then I found the story of Scheherazade and *The Arabian Nights*. I couldn't stop reading, or falling in love with how that one girl, as a result of all that she studied, all that she had remembered, was able to save her own life and transform a killing-machine-of-a-king and become queen. If Scheherazade could do that, so could I. S.c.h.e.h.e.r.a.z.a.d.e.

For months I read everything I could get me hands on. I also demanded that everyone around me call me Scheherazade. "S.c.h.e.h.e.r.a.z.a.d.e." Scheherazade I became.

Compliment Him On A Body Part

The file cabinet containing all of the case-files of the resident's histories, was kept in the on-site psychiatrist's office. Morris was his name. The cabinet was locked. Always. Morris took the key with him each night, after work. A hundred times I'd watched him sit back in his armchair, one leg across the other and twirling his pencil between his lip and moustache. Sometimes, he'd rock back and forth. I'd speak. He'd jot something down. Once. I asked.

"What are you writing about?" Curious. "Just a few notes," Morris replied. I did not believe him. "Can I read what you wrote about me?" I was serious. "I don't know, *can* you?" He thought himself quite funny. I thought him quite not so funny.

Lolita had confided in me that Morris could be persuaded to see things "your way" if you'd be willing to come off as nice. Syrupy. All I'd have to do was compliment him on a body part. Apparently Morris had a hang up about the front of his hair, the way you could see straight through it to the back of his head, so to say to him "Man, your hair is blazin' today, Morris," could've made things he wrote down go in my favor. I wasn't interested.

Cabinet

It was a busy Monday, and two days after I'd heard about Gwen, and she was still the only person on my call list. So, when Lolita had asked for the screwdriver in order to tighten the screws on her window shades I made sure to be around when she finished using it. Once done, she placed the tool back into the custodian's basket, and signed it in, again, on the clipboard that hung on the wall in the counselor's office. I slipped in right behind her and grabbed the screwdriver before anyone had time to take it back to the tool shed and lock it up.

I half expected someone to have seen me, to have sat all day on the fact that I'd not only stolen personal property, but I'd committed the infraction involving something which belonged to the facility. If caught it would have carried outrageous penalties; no outings, swimming, level demotion. I imagined that whoever it was enjoyed biding their time, storing up until the right moment they'd want to bust me. Every resident got busted at one point for something or another. If I were to get caught, they'd laugh, one after the other, get all hyped-up on the scene of it all like orangutans. Anyway. Nothing like that happened. So.

Just before midnight, and at least forty-five minutes before the night shift workers handed over the keys, and the *Day's Notes* to the graveyard worker, Edith, I stood in front of the beige file cabinet in Morris' office. The bathroom window had been left unlocked. Lucky for me. I'd planned on breaking it anyway with a knee-high basketball sock over my hand. Mafia style. I placed the head of the screwdriver between the cabinet lock bar and a partially opened drawer. I pulled until the drawer bent enough for me to see the files hanging on the glider. It was too easy finding my name, I was the only resident whose name ended in "O." I was the last name in the bunch.

I read a brief letter from a social worker I didn't remember having:

Dear Gwen Forde, MSW:

I am following up on the conversation we had about Regina. As I hand this case off to you I want to summarize a few thoughts. I agree that a residential placement sounds like the best approach, at this time.

Because Regina has poor internal control, a firm well--defined and consistent structure is most helpful to her. She responded best when the limits were clearly known to her and were enforced. Besides this type of structure, Regina has strong unmet dependency needs. She sees herself as having made all the decisions about her various living circumstances, i.e., with her foster grandmother, in Texas, her mother, whereabouts unknown and her father, who resides in Richmond, California, but refuses to maintain contact with his daughter.

Therefore, she feels responsible for many of the unpleasant circumstances in her life. Regina has a need for a great amount of adult attention, and she needs a space to calm her inner life apart from the pressures of group living. Furthermore, consistency and firmness in limit setting gives her the security that she is cared for.

[redacted] M.A
Social Worker
November 18, 1976

The psychological report from Dr. Cohen started out as:

December 18th, 1978

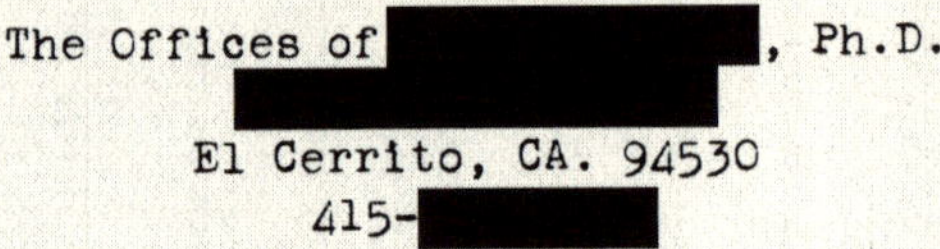
The Offices of ██████, Ph.D.
██████
El Cerrito, CA. 94530
415-██████

Patient, a young black female, possibly beautiful, arrived this afternoon, to my office, for her appointment in a timely manner. There was no noticeable evidence of a patois, and upon further inquiry I found that patient presented, dialectically, as well as could be expected considering she is a Negro girl of a particular background.

Patient-- (16), arrived dressed in tight-fitting black jumpsuit with bell-bottoms which accentuated her body possibly suggesting a peculiar type of sensuality: one such that might be expected from a woman ten years the senior of patients age.

Although patient exhibited behaviors consistent with someone who is intent on seduction or charm, I do not believe her intent was to neither seduce, nor charm...

I tried reading at the pace of my heartbeat and could not keep up. My fingers ran over the tops of pages clamped together with staples, large paper clips, each packed to the margins with words that had very little meaning for me at that time, the diagnosis of Borderline Personality Disorder, Oppositional Disorder, and Immaturity Disorder. Manic Depressive. According to what I'd read, all those labels made me out to be a doomed laboratory rat just waiting to see how everyone was going to fix what was wrong with me.

I didn't know exactly *what* I was looking for, but I knew I was running out of time and I wanted to find out what Morris had to say about me, I wanted to know if he was talking behind my back, telling lies.

And then I found a Xerox copy of a letter:

October 12th, 1978

Dear Punkin!

I'm sending this letter to you through Gwen Forde. I pray that things are well with you, that you are, as you said doing your very best and letting the people at Guideways get to know you-showing them the Regina I know and LOVE!

Regina, it will be up to you how you adjust at Guideways, which will determine when you will hear from me again. Many people who also care about you have told me that it will make it hard for you to adjust, and settle in if we keep writing, talking and seeing each other until you have established roots in your new home. I'm counting on you to let yourself settle in and do your very best to let this placement work. Those old key words: It's up to you honey. Until I am given permission I will not write you nor will I accept any phone calls and I will not see you. You know Punkin; a period of silence and separation is a very small part of time when you look at a lifetime. I know with all my heart that we will be close friends our whole life long. I am behind you Punkin, rooting for you all the way.

Some things we must face alone, but I am always with you in spirit. You are always in my heart. You need to discuss things with your social worker, share your thoughts and feelings, confide in the staff there and make new friendships.

As you said, "Think about your actions," and the consequences of those actions before you act. Do your very best to work on those basics sweetheart. It doesn't happen overnight, have patience. Each day is a new start; a new beginning. You may have to start new each day. I have faith in you; if you put your mind to it and keep plugging away it will eventually happen.

One suggestion is to each night ask yourself if you have done your very best that day; see where changes can be made, and then try again. It takes concentration and willpower; you can do it if you really want to!

Another suggestion is to ask yourself what nice thing you have done for someone else that day. You are very good at this, it's one of your special qualities that make you, YOU!

I keep remembering that you are in God's hands; the very best hands, and that you have decided to settle in, and do your very best. Once you put your mind and will behind something, Regina you do your very best, the rest is up to God. Trust Him, Regina; He loves you more than anyone.

With All My Love,
Jeanne K. Kerr
Ms. J.K. Kerr

If You'd Like To Make A Call, Please Hang Up, And Try Your Call Again

The pay phone in the resident's T.V. room was bolted to the wall straight across from the counselor's office. I'd forgotten how long I'd been in Morris' office reading through the file, forgotten to take note of when I'd heard the wheels of Edith's cherried-out El Camino *Impala* spit gravel as it turned into the driveway, I forgot to close the file cabinet. Didn't think to bring change with me to make a call.

I picked up the office receiver and dialed Jeanne's number. "Miss Kerr? It's me, Regina." She'd picked up on the third ring. "Hi Sweetheart," she said. "What time is it? Are you okay?"

Barely able to contain myself, I cupped my hand over my mouth and whispered into the receiver.

"When you coming to see me?" "Do you have permission to speak with me, Regina?" "How come you haven't called?" "It's after 2 AM." "Are you coming— "Sweetheart, I can't talk with you." "I gotta know when you're coming" "I have to go sweetie. I'm… sorry."

S.H.U.

Later that morning.

Arms thick as bologna logs, hands, the size of a Rawlings Alpha catcher's mitt, Fatman gripped my wrist and ankle. He dug his nails into my flesh, squeezed and kneaded until it felt as if I were going to pop right out of me. With back and forth motions he pulled me from my bed, out of my room, down the hallway, and used my body to sweep away everything in our path: rugs, chairs, and forgotten about shoes. I knew where we were going.

I was a windshield wiper. He was a restraining staff committed to reinforcing the rules. We tripped over the plastic tables, where the rest of the residents sat with inhaled faces fallen in at the mouth from eating watery, powdered eggs, and cold *Wonder* white sliced bread.

"What are y'all lookin' at? I yelled. He swung me. We do-si-doed. "I can call anybody I want, man!" I screamed.

The way the other residents sat there, not helping, nothing staring back at me from behind their sunken eyes, reminded me of forgotten about old people in a convalescent home in wheel-less wheel chairs.

I'd earned that phone call.

That dumb-■ song from *Mr. Rogers' Neighborhood* wafted from the bulging eye of the Zenith TV, as Fatman raked my hundred-pound body across the tiled floors; their splintered and chipped edges so sharp nobody's bare feet were safe, even with shoes on, let alone my legs dangling from shorts. No matter how hard I tried that day was not going to be a wonderful one in my neighborhood.

I imagined chunks of reddish brown pieces of me spackled the places where the tiles used to be. "I earned that call, man!" "Forget y'all! I ain't going in there!" "I ain't going." Fatman kept hauling me through the room. I kept resisting. Fighting. "I didn't ask to come here no way," I said, struggling against his strength.

I tore at him, the plastic checkered tabletop, and the plates, crashed to the floor trying to hold on to something. Anything. Someone's leg. She kicked my hands off her. Went back to eating.

I became so slippery with food and sweat from kicking and fighting. Fatman let go of my arm long enough to lift that silver gym teacher whistle to his lips and blew panic and spit all over the place.

I flipped around and sank my teeth into his calf. He howled. He was a wounded beast. Game changed.

"We've got a biter! Need backup NOW!" Fatman screamed into a two-way radio. Somebody should've told him. He pulled back. Too late. I was a rabid dog who wasn't about to let go of him. They'd have to kill me first.

Startled, he kicked and batted at the air. But like a pit-bull, my jaw sank deeper into him. With the sticky palm of his hand he smashed down onto the side of my face. His fingers pried into my lips, clawed my gums, my teeth, my grip.

Fatman screamed and danced around as far as his free leg would allow him to move, then he toppled to the ground. Someone wound my plaited hair round their hand and jerked me from behind, while another somebody bum-rushed their entire hand inside my mouth.

My head yanked back, my jowl unlocked, Fatman cried out like a kicked-in-the-belly beast and through the splay of fingers, I watched him palm-and-slide, palm-and-slide his big body all the way down the hall.

Maryanne-the-yes-man had her arm around my throat, in a chokehold. I tried to kick my way out of it, but she dragged me down anyway. I flailed and she snatched my black self down a flight of twenty-two stairs. I lost a footie, the one with the yellow pom-pom on the back, the one Miss Kerr had given me the last time I saw her.

I couldn't get loose. Breath was hard to come by. Somebody grabbed my feet, foot cuffed them, and wheel-barrowed me forward, and down. Down to the last step.

I knew what was coming. I knew where they were taking me. I'd seen many girls lose days folded up into embryos for days on end after being released from the security-housing unit. I'd heard that once inside the SHU box, all hell was going to break loose. Once inside the SHU box there was no coming out until I could "learn to self-soothe." Once inside, there would be no me. No God. I would not remember that God so loved anyone, least of all me.

Maryanne-the-yes-man barked at someone to "open the door!"

"I'll be good, now!" I screamed. "Good. Just don't put me in there. Please, don't!" I begged. Five, six, maybe even seven sets of hands pushed me into a room no bigger than a burying plot. A blurry group of gowns and pajamas crowded the stairwell. “Back to your rooms NOW!” Maryanne-the-yes-man yelled.

“I’ll die in here,” I cried, and tried to ram past the staff members’ bodies that blocked the doorway. They held onto one another’s torsos and shoulders. They wove a thick net.

“I’m gone die,” I said and continued to push against the hands arms, and legs that jammed my only way out. I rammed hard. Hard against them. Hard against them. Someone pushed back with such force I was knocked down, and onto the concrete floor. My breath caught like a giant fist, in my throat.

I scrambled to get up onto my hands and knees in time to reach for the door, as it slammed shut. It barely missed my fingers.

“I… cain’t breath.” I pounded with both hands. “God? Somebody, HELP ME!” I screamed. Until I couldn’t. “You’ll get as good as you get. Now bring it down, way down!”

There was no handle. No windows. No air. The ceiling plunged towards me. The walls pressed in. My fingernails scraped against the floor. I was a dog tap dancing on concrete floors. I scrambled down into the space where the door and floor met. I opened my mouth to scream into the slit of light barely showing through, but nothing came out. I was beyond the place of tears and everything was upside down, I needed air, I sucked, and sucked and sucked for air, wishing. Hoping. Wanting.

“Ruby…”

Antipsychotic

"Next," the nurse called out. In two month's time I'd messed myself up good from being the first to get my chores done, to get into to the van, the pool, the line for dinner, to being the last in line to throw back meds from a tiny, white, pleated *Dixie* cup.

The nurse. Morris. Phyllis. Gwen. All the adults who oversaw my care made it their business to try and convince me that my destructive behavior was not my fault. They told me that my body had deficiencies that wouldn't allow my brain to function normally, like "regular" kids my age. I was told that in order to stay at Guideways, and not be terminated or transferred to a low-level psychiatric ward for adolescents, I'd have to agree to a daily regimen of psychotropic meds. Most all the residents, except Lolita, relied upon one cocktail after another of prescribed medications to aid them in managing their ability to "get through" the day.

I didn't want the meds. I took them because I also didn't want to end up needing drugs to make it through my life, and I figured if I took them, I'd fix whatever was broken inside me. I had dreams. I was good with hair, I had vocals, was told I was "pretty enough to be a model." I imagined myself a ballet dancer. It always ran through my mind what Miss Kerr had said "You can become anything you want." I still believed it.

Day after day I popped two small, orange Thorazine* pills. When

I was done popping Thorazine I popped two small brown Mellaril* pills, and when I was done popping Mellaril I popped a small pink Stellazine* pill, and when I was done popping Stellazine I popped a large peach capsule of Lithium*

---

*Thioridazine is an antipsychotic medicine called a phenothiazine. It works by changing the actions of chemicals in your brain. Thioridazine is used to treat schizophrenia and other antipsychotic conditions. Thioridazine is usually given after other antipsychotic medicines have been tried without success.

*Mellaril is used to treat certain mental/mood disorders, e.g., schizophrenia. This medication helps you to think more clearly, feel less nervous, and take part in everyday life. It can also help prevent suicide in people likely to harm themselves and reduce aggression and the desire to hurt others.

*Stellazine rifluoperazine is an anti-psychotic medicine in a group of drugs called phenothiazines (FEEN-oh-THYE-a-zeens). It works by changing the actions of chemicals in your brain. Trifluoperazine is used to treat anxiety or psychotic disorders such as schizophrenia.

*Lithium acts on a person's central nervous system (brain and spinal cord). Doctors don't know exactly how lithium works to stabilize a person's mood, but it is thought to help strengthen nerve cell connections in brain regions that are involved in regulating mood, thinking and behavior.

*Cogentin is used to treat symptoms of Parkinson's disease or involuntary movements due to the side effects of certain psychiatric drugs (antipsychotics such as (Thorazine and Mellaril). Cogentin belongs to a class of medications called anticholinergics that work by blocking a certain natural substance (acetylcholine). This helps decrease muscle stiffness, sweating, and the production of saliva, and helps improve walking ability in people with Parkinson's disease.

Take Them You'll Be Fine

One morning I awoke trembling. I could barely stand; my hands couldn't hold onto a glass of milk without shaking.

"I can't stop shaking," I told the nurse, my hands visibly moved involuntarily. She gave me the cup of pills. "Take them, you'll be fine." I left her and walked over to Morris' office.

"Look at me," I told him, as I stood obviously unable to control my body movements. He sat there. Crossed leg. Twirled pencil. Stared. And stared. I was a wild animal. He sat there. Crossed leg. Twirled pencil. Stared. And stared. I was a circus freak. He sat there. Crossed leg. Twirled pencil. Stared. And stared. I was a minute away from taking that pencil from him. He sat there. Crossed leg. Twirled pencil. Stared. And stared.

"It'll take time for the medicine to take affect," Morris said. "Just you wait, pretty soon you'll be a whole new "You."

To Do Things On It's Own

Another hot day at Guideways. Morris and Phyllis thought it a good idea for me to get out of the house, get an "airing out," they'd called it. I'd gone through a series of repeated hospital visits where I had to be injected with Cogentin to counteract almost swallowing my tongue, shitting myself, loss of tongue control. Drooling. Swimming would be good for my body, they said.

Miss Kerr had taught me to freestyle across the entire length of an Olympic-sized pool at Heather Farms: a local public park in Walnut Creek. We'd switch it up between there and the "Y" in Pleasant Hill. For whatever the reason, I hadn't readily taken to the pool at Guideways. Maybe it was the way we had to ask each and every time anyone wanted to swim, maybe it was the cold cyclone fence that traveled the circumference of the pool and was secured with a bowling ball sized padlock, making it feel more like a water treat ment plant, a giant petri dish, or an aquarium where we were the freaks people were meant to come and oogle at, but didn't. Maybe it was because Miss Kerr wasn't there to do cannonballs with me. Jack knife. Somersaults off the diving board.

I'd swam a few laps when out of nowhere my entire body began to do things on it's own. Each attempt to propel my arms simultaneously in order to get from the six-foot side of the pool to the shallow end resulted in my splashing the water like someone with a palsy might. My arms and legs became heavier, faster. The more I tried to warn the staff member in charge of watching me that something was not right, the more paralyzed I became. My tongue quit working. Words slurred. My head twisted on it's own as if it were trying to get a three sixty view of the situation, as if I were Linda Blair in the *Exorcist*.

The staff member waved me away. "Stop being silly," he yelled.

No sooner did my brain transmit to my legs to kick, and to my arms to propel or else drown, that it became evident: I was already drowning.

I never remembered being pulled from the pool, the whirring sound of the ambulance, the gurney, the breathing machines, tubes. It took the medic nearly fifteen minutes, a team of emergency room doctors and nurses another thirty, to figure out that I was not a Parkinson's patient, but instead, a child who had been—yet again—over medicated.

I awoke in a pile of my own bile, my own urine. Feces.

A male nurse grabbed a handful of my butt-cheek, pinched it up into a mound of flesh and shoved a four-inch needle loaded with Cogentin into me.

Within minutes, my tongue, a retractable tape measure slipped back into my mouth.

Using the back of my hand I wiped the slobber-vomit cocktail from the corners of my mouth, my chin. My fingers, which earlier had involuntarily frozen in the wickedness of a witch's hands, the fierceness of gnarly tree roots, slowly returned to the hands of my seventeen-year-old self. I didn't know it then, but I had been to Parkinson's disease and back way before my time.

Man

"Man, y'all gotta take me off this mess," I told Morris, Phyllis. Gwen. "Man, y'all gotta take me off this mess," I told Morris, Phyllis. Gwen. "Man, y'all gotta take me off this mess," I told Morris, Phyllis. Gwen. "Man, y'all gotta take me off this mess," I told Morris, Phyllis. Gwen. "Man, y'all gotta take me off this mess," I told Morris, Phyllis. Gwen. "Man, y'all gotta take me off this mess," I told Morris, Phyllis. Gwen. "Man, y'all gotta take me off this mess," I told Morris, Phyllis. Gwen. "Man, y'all gotta take me off this mess," I told Morris, Phyllis. Gwen.

Each morning, the nurse handed me the small, pleated white cup and watched me take my meds.

"Man, y'all gotta take me off this mess," I told Morris, Phyllis. Gwen. "Man, y'all gotta take me off this mess," I told Morris, Phyllis. Gwen. "Man, y'all gotta take me off this mess," I told Morris, Phyllis. Gwen. "Man, y'all gotta take me off this mess," I told Morris, Phyllis. Gwen.

Each morning, the nurse handed me the small, pleated white cup…

"Man, y'all gotta take me off this mess," I told Morris, Phyllis. Gwen. "Man, y'all gotta take me off this mess,"

Each morning, the nurse handed me…

Manic

All anyone had to do, was take a minute, and calculate the number of times I'd been driven, ambulanced, and rushed to the local hospital to have my body pumped full of medication to counteract the adverse side-effects of yet another failed medication regimen. All they had to do was pay attention to what those drugs were doing to me, taking from me: my ability to think for myself, feed, clothe, wipe myself. All the hopefulness that melted into listlessness that hung in strands of slobber from the side of my sagging mouth.

All anyone had to do, and that was the disgrace of it; was unlock those files they kept on me, and all those other girls who shuffled around Guideways numbed, dulled, so far gone we bore the brunt end of the cliché: *the lights are on, but nobody's home.* Social workers, judges and counselors alike could've worked better together to figure out why we had no visitors, no calls, no real friends, to call friends, and make it a point to get us peopled-up in such a way that the talons of grief would have no way to clutch hold of our young hearts and further rip to shreds what was left of our already-to-much-for-a-child-to-bear-brokenness.

All anyone had to do, was imagine me, back then, as an adolescent girl entitled to my pain, my loss, my grief. I was affected by my compounded traumas; leaving Miss Kerr, losing my freedoms. What about my hopes, my dreams, my want for a mother, and not just any kind of mother they constantly threw my way to try on like an old hand me down, but the one who I had something in common with, one who had a vested interest in my future and well being, one who chose me as I was choosing her, one who wanted me for a daughter as much as I imagined she could be my mother.

All anybody had to do, really, was search into their own hearts, their own experiences with family, acceptance, belonging and togetherness, failure and loss and imagine for us something more dignified, something more humane that shifted the blame placed on the victims—us girls—who were already too beaten down to crawl back up the bucket of our collective nothingness into an almost probable future of failure, and all anybody had to do was approach us from a place of worthiness because I, we, they also wanted to know what it felt like to give and receive love. That was all anyone had to do. If they wanted to shift their perceptions and realized we needed solutions of the heart, not solutions that line the pocketbooks.

Porgy & Bess

The theatre department at Shasta Community College had placed an ad in a local dailies announcing the casting call for the play, Porgy and Bess. I knew nothing about Gershwin, his play, or the music but the ad was clear: they were looking for a black female and male between the ages of seventeen and twenty-one to play the parts of Porgy and Bess. I fit that bill. I believed back then that I was the only black person within a one-hundred-mile radius of Redding. There were no black counselors, we had no black neighbors and anytime the ambulance or the police showed up at Guideways—which was all too frequent—none of them were black. I saw no black folks at the mall, at the Red Lion Hotel restaurant were we'd go and devour deep fried shrimp the size of a baseball at the first of the month if the county had paid it's boarding home wage for us, on time. I'd caught wind about how a few other residents were getting close to emancipating. What they were going to do? Where would they go once they turned eighteen? I was afraid of that word—"emancipating."* I was a slave.

---

*Unshackling of minors in such a way that minor is released from control by his or her parents or guardians, and the parents or guardians are freed from any and all responsibility toward the child.

College was still my number one choice, but I hadn't been able to convince anyone I had what it took to get in, stay there, and graduate with a suitable future career; maybe become a singer, an actress, or a social worker? Not even when I won several hundred dollars from the ladies over at the Redding Junior League for getting straight "A's" from the reading boxes, did anybody think much of what I could do. Those J.L. ladies didn't know that I really wasn't doing real schoolwork and that a kindergartner could've probably whipped me to the finish with some of those lessons. They were however, those ladies, fascinated by the fact that I did write the letter nominating myself to receive the prize money, along with a year's supply of Coca-Cola. I liked that they liked that I could do that, and so I wanted to do more things like that—win—in order to get people's attention.

The way I tended to look at things was: the casting call, not so unlike the Junior League contest, was fate's way of leading me to my destiny. It was, maybe, God's way of telling me to get out of Guideways as quickly as I could.

I didn't bother to ask a staff member to give me a lift down to the place where the auditions were being held. I sneaked out the backdoor, past the locked pool area and ran up the hill to the 7-Eleven store on Dana Drive. I waited there, leaning on a side wall till I saw a lady I thought looked nice enough to thumb a ride from; she had to be young-looking, and smile at me when I gave her eye contact. It only took seconds for several people to flat-out avoid my gaze, but then, a white girl in her twenties, smiled back at me as I walked past her car as she opened the door. She pulled the Volkswagen bug out of the parking lot and I quickly held my thumb out, and walked backwards in the direction I was headed praying she was going my way.

I'd heard the horror stories about young girls taking rides from a car full of men and were then found chopped up, dropped off, or never to be found again. The Zodiac killer was still on the loose then, as well. That struck righteous fear in me. But. I was young. Bold. Idealistic. I believed that all I had to do was tell myself to never let something like that happen, to never take rides from strange men offering up coins, or lollipops, or cotton candy potentially laced with razor blades who would "swear to God," that my mother had sent him (Of course in my case that would've been the dead give-away.) Even though I thought that hitchhiking was for white people and that maybe the chick wouldn't turn; I kept walking back as she waited for the coast to clear to pullout of the driveway. She stopped.

"What can you sing?," asked one of the two people who sat at a folding table in front of me. The white chick had dropped me off at the local high school—Enterprise—I believe it was. I had no idea that I was supposed to have a song prepared, and the only one I knew is one I'd heard on the radio some time back by Nina Simone. I got through the first verse of *Young, Gifted and Black*, before I was stopped, and handed a page of the play script to take home and get myself acquainted with.

"Are you familiar with *Porgy and Bess?*" The casting director asked, and I told him, "No," that I wasn't. "It's okay," he said. You did great. "Are you available for after-school rehearsals?" "Yes!" I answered. More than anything I was so happy to be able to say yes to something that had nothing to do with Guideways.

It wasn't *just* because I had sneaked off to audition for the part that I wasn't allowed to have my "Broadway moment," it was also because no one at Guideways had ever done such a thing, because no one in town could know that I was an orphan, ward of the court, a teenager. I felt, at that time that, it was also because Guideways was just as invested in my becoming a nobody as Gwen was.

I understood this: It took a gang of folks to pump me full of drugs, keep me off course, let me know I didn't have what it took to go the distance. It took only one to tell me "You can be whatever you want..." It was all a matter of what I wanted to believe. They may've kept Miss Kerr from me, but like that girl Dorothy, with me or not: Miss Kerr was the reflection of myself outside myself. Miss Kerr was my Toto.

Milk Vat

By the time the green S.E Rykoff truck, (tattooed with the slogan "Eat Out More Often"), pulled out from the back of the Guideways' kitchen, I'd already saved-up enough pills to tranquilize a small herd of sheep. Thorazine. Mellaril. Lithium.

Each time the nurse handed me the daily dose of 10, 20 or 50 milligrams of whatever they were serving me that day from the *Dixie Cup*, I'd stuff the capsules into the seams of my gum line, or plant them at the back of my mouth, beneath my tongue. I had a month of savings.

I had a plan. Worked on it for weeks after the swimming pool incident, after pleading and begging to be taken off the meds. I waited for the night shift to exchange keys with Edith.

I knew where Edith was at all times. Edith was a large woman and when she walked her thighs crushed the threads from her polyester, pull-on slacks.

Once Edith made her rounds to the other side of the facility, I was up. Earlier that day I'd recovered the pills from the throat of the tree stump where I'd buried them. I'd enclosed them in Saran wrap, and for extra security used a red rubber band to prevent them from getting wet and or dissolving.

Pills in hand, I tiptoed down the corridor from my bedroom to the kitchen.

From my sock, I grabbed hold of the butter knife I'd saved from dinner. I shoved the butt end, the thickest part of the knife, into the space between the U-shaped shackle and the body of the padlock.

The door housing the milk vat was always locked. We weren't allowed to drink milk, juice or water anytime we wanted. Such luxuries were saved for meals and counselor-sanctioned snack times.

I gave myself ten minutes to pop that lock. It took one. Once I came up with the idea, I'd spent the last month practicing how to break the lock. I'd used the money I'd earned from the Redding Junior League to buy a pack of locks the same size as the ones used in the kitchen.

I placed the deformed lock on the counter. I opened the front of the milk vat. Using the knife, I slit the top of the gigantic plastic bag, which held a week's worth of milk.

I pulled the pills from the waistband of my underwear, unwrapped them and dumped all thirty capsules into the milk vat that the entire facility drank from.

The poison, floated on top of the white liquid. I didn't need to watch them melt into the milk—the way they'd floated on my saliva, and then dissolved into my blood.

Spite

Although I never let on, to anyone, Edith, the in-a-pinch graveyard worker and I had a thing. Sometimes. When a drug wreaked havoc on my conscious and I couldn't make sense of where I was or what was going on, I'd slip out of bed and scooch on over to the counselor's office, where more often than not I found Edith sitting there, smoking a Marlboro Light, talking to her husband, Larry, who thought it smart to have swastikas inked all over his skinny arms. He was the Laurel to her Hardy.

He'd said, "Hey there, Jungle Bunny," Larry did, the first time I met him when he'd driven Edith by the facility to pick up her paycheck and she'd made the mistake of introducing us. "Next time, 'Spear Chucker,' was how he said goodbye.

Although I didn't understand—then—that all things Larry pointed to bigotry and an in your face abhorrence for anyone who wasn't a white supremacist, I would, later when I asked Gwen if I could stay with Edith over a Christmas holiday. I told her Edith's husband seemed nice enough although he'd called me interesting names, one's I'd never heard before, but something about them didn't feel quite right, especially when they both laughed (or snickered in Edith's case.)

I repeated the names:

Jungle bunny.

Spear chucker.

Gwen gave me that "You've got to be kidding me stare," until I understood what it must've felt like to be the dumbest person alive. Unbeknownst to me, I was. Beggars couldn't be choosey. I was looking out for myself, and I needed a place to stay over the holidays. "What can I do you for, chickpea?" Edith asked. Her dentures were so evenly cut they looked like a pair of wind-up, chattering teeth. I stood in the doorway. Thought about how I would break what I had done, to her. "C'mon spit it out." Edith said. "I put a month's worth of meds in the milk vat." I liked Edith.

When I won the money from the junior league for getting good grades I'd used a portion of it to get Edith a gift. Miss Kerr had encouraged me, in the letter I snuck and read, to let folks get to know the me that she loved. It was hard for me to do that, let people get to know me. I didn't want Miss Kerr to think that I'd found someone to replace her, that I didn't like her as much and in return she'd stop liking me, or get her feelings hurt. So, I forced myself to try and like Edith.

A few times, when I couldn't sleep she let me come into the staff office and sit on her lap until I fell off to sleep. I can't imagine what that must've looked like, a big girl like me sitting on a grown woman's lap. She'd sleepwalk me back to my room. Anyway. Edith looked like she needed a new pair of shoes. I bought them for her. A pair of those *Famolare* "rollercoasters" in brown. I got her the slip-on ones so that she wouldn't have to bend all the way over. I thought the shoes would prevent her from wobbling when she walked.

I told her about the drugs because I didn't want her or the other residents to suffer any more than they needed to. My intention was never to really hurt anyone. I was just in a rage that no one thought enough of me to listen. My seventeen-year-old logic wanted an eye-for-an-eye. But not really.

Terminated

ter·mi·nate
/ˈtərmə, nāt/
verb
past tense: **terminated**; past participle: **terminated**
1. bring to an end.
"he was advised to terminate the contract"
synonyms: bring to an end, abort, curtail bring to an end/close/conclusion, put an end to, wind up, wrap up, discontinue, cease, kill, cut short, ax;

Me, and the garbage bag I used (packed with even fewer things than I had upon my arrival to Guideways), sat in the Redding Municipal Airport terminal waiting to leave Redding. I was hot, but not as hot as I would've been in the TV room at Guideways, no air conditioning, and passing time till the next dose of "you ain't-worth-a-nickel" to be served up in a paper cup. I was satisfied to sit and await for the arrival of the Hughes Airwest flight that was going to take me into San Francisco.

Gwen had refused to make the drive to come and pick me up "one more time," from a "failed" placement that I could've made work. The way I saw it? She really hadn't done that much picking me up. If she'd remembered correctly she would've seen that I did most of the picking me up and leaving by all the running away, I'd done. I'd been working with her, actually. As far as failing the placement was concerned, that was her way of looking at it, not mine. On the other hand, I could see her reasoning that if I was old enough to be so strong-minded, I should've been old enough to face the consequences of my actions. As long as no one beat me, I was fine with that.

I had no idea where I was headed, what would happen once I arrived, if there'd be more names to learn to only have to forget, more staff to kiss-up to, more games to play where the odds of winning would never be in my favor. And though I sat in that waiting room my t-shirt waterlogged, hanging from my skin, my lifeless bangs sticking straight up from my hairline and my hand so wet the garbage bag became hard to hold onto, even so—I still managed to rustle up a true sense of relief of never having to return to Redding, to that squat, puss colored house where erasure, disguised as rehabilitation, hijacked the hopes, and dreams of so many young and troubled girls' and obliterated them like paper dolls in a hurricane. And unlike them I was unwilling to be forever lost and lifeless in the background of a psychotropic nightmare.

You'll Be Here Until...

Gwen met me at San Francisco International. As to be expected, we didn't exchange words of excitement regarding seeing one another. A nod between the two of us stood for what was unspoken. It had been almost seven months since I'd seen Gwen, maybe more. I slid into the passengers' seat, buckled up, and quickly anchored into the separateness that held us both.

I knew better than to ask questions, because questions required answers and answers—from me, to Gwen—demanded I have a solid reason for why I "threatened" to poison an entire facility with the very meds that were meant to poison me. I would've had to work hard at convincing the same person who'd secretly solicited my father's signature in favor of Guideways administering psychotropic meds to a teenager that what I *really* needed was to be held, encouraged, granted the benefit of the doubt that I was actually incapable of managing the emotions and traumatic experiences the adults in my life had not been successful with.

I know now, that those things take time, understanding and considerations towards change. But also, I wanted to be extend ed the common courtesy of not ever having to be tossed onto a cold, naked, floor with no way out and forced to shut down the emotional turmoil on a dime, or else have to suffer more for it. Especially a child. I felt no different at Guideways than if I'd been with Lula Mae when she'd say "Shut the ████ up before I give you something to *really* cry about." Granted, I was not an easy child, I see that. What I wanted then, is for Gwen, or someone to help me through the darkness of the indescribable. I wanted someone to be Annie Sullivan to my Helen Keller. Instead, I felt that I was the pariah to their piety.

That day, on our way to San Francisco, when the silence was broken, it was Gwen who stepped up. "You'll be here until I find a placement for you in San Francisco, Regina." It would take weeks for me to unpack my bag, believe that my next placement would be one where I might exhale. Feel the ground beneath my feet.

Prim & Proper

Jezebel June's house sat in the center of a cul-de-sac near Mac -donald Boulevard in a section of Richmond I hadn't known when I lived there that first time with my father. Four and a half years had passed since I was last in the same town where Tom lived. It would've been nice to look up my friend from the shelter, Valencia. Lolita was slated to emancipate from Guide-ways but I'd have no way of reaching either one of them; that was the life of a foster child. We were the original rolling stones, we didn't take names or numbers as we rolled through.

"You can call me, June," said a beautiful black woman, after Gwen left. Her skin was more similar to mine than I'd ever seen on any-one, other than my mother. She had a glow, June did.

"Don't mind Miss Gwen," she continued, "I've been working with her for a long while now and every time she drops one of you kids off she says the same thing: "You can address your new fos-ter parent as Ms. June." June mocked Gwen's prim and proper mannerisms. "I'm no 'Ms.', she said with a playful edge. We both laughed small laughs. I smiled a bit longer than I had in a long while. Miss June seemed easy going. Something on my insides recognized another something: I felt suddenly at ease with June. She reminded me of Miss Kerr.

June showed me to my room. But first, we had to walk a flight of stairs to get there. Along the way, to the right and nailed to the wall were twelve framed photographs of Jesus in various stages of hardship. I stopped and paid rapt attention to the twelfth picture, the one where Jesus' feet, and hands were nailed to the cross he'd been forced to carry.

"I see you know about them Stations of the Cross?" June asked. I didn't know the photos by name, but I figured out the story the pictures told. Something softened in my heart. It had been a while since I'd been eye-to-eye with the son of God. "I put these here pictures up to remind me to think good on my own mama. Like so many of you kids, us grown people have problems with our people too. That's why I try and help as many of you as I can, you see. I walk these stations everyday, up, down, and up again, that way I won't forget to be humble."

"Thank you," I told June and went into my room. I checked beneath the bed, inside the small closet, gauged the distance between the roof and the ground, the front door and my room, the back door. Unlike that Preachers' house, June's seemed better suited for Jesus. Something about the way she explained *why* she did things the way she did made sense to me. She talked to me like she understood that I understood. I appreciated that. I allowed myself to give June a chance and at least stay the night.

Sodom & Gomorrah

The next morning was November 18th, 1978. The television was so loud it jolted me awake. I got dressed and went downstairs.

What looked like black bodies scattered and splayed across the screen as if they'd rained down from Heaven, as if they laid prone amongst large arms locked with small arms locked with thick arms and slim one's laced and sealed as if in silent contemplation, as if in prayer, just so happened to be: black bodies scattered and splayed across the screen and small arms locked with thick arms, intertwined with slim one's. They weren't lying there as if in supplication, as if beseeching God one last time for one more chance. Lord. They weren't doing that because they were all dead.

June paced the floor between the kitchen and the living room. The news reported the incident of the Guyana massacre and I reached for the bag that held the bottle of my liquid Thorazine. I'd decided I wouldn't give June a hard time about taking it.

"Can you tell me where I can get a spoon?" I asked June. She seemed jitterier than she had the night before. "Hallelujah!" June shouted out, "The Lord will not be merciful to sinners I say! You see here what happens to sinners?" she asked pointing at the television screen. "The Lord will not be merciful. You cannot, I say, drink from the chalice of the world, and dwell in the house of the Lord. No child in this house can be on drugs. If you on drugs and you're in this house you got's to go."

I was confused.

"Are you sure?" I asked. The Hallelujah woman placed the palm of her right hand on my forehead and shouted: "Li'l lamb of God, as of now...I say as of right now... I say...as of right here in this minute and by the Glory of God... you are no longer on them drugs. You are no longer afflicted with the sickness of disobedience. Look what the drugs have done. Them drugs is of them white folks. See what that white man has gone and done? He's done made believers out of the lost. He drugged them believers with the Kool-Aid of Satan. I say Satan-nanananananana. Give your life over to Christ Jeeeesus!"

Gwen had nowhere else to send me. June gave her an ultimatum: either drop the meds, or drop me someplace else. That day, I dropped Thorazine cold turkey. I spent a day or two vomiting, had diarrhea, and going up and down those stairs made my head spin. Didn't matter. I never looked back.

I vowed to never forget Jezebel June.

"This Here, Regina?"

Just like that. Out of nowhere the call came. A man's voice. Deep. Gruff. Talked as if he knew me, first hand, as if suddenly I was someone who counted.

I still lived with June, still waited for an opening at some place in San Francisco.

"Yeah, it's me, who's this?" I didn't know any men other than Tom. "This here, Lebanon Johnson. I'm calling on behalf of Ruby Carmichael. You know who that is?"

Ruby? It took a moment for memory to catch the name, put a face to the name, register in my mind that someone other than me had spoken my mother's name in a way that made the moment feel as if I was time traveling while standing still.

"She with you?" I asked Mr. Lebanon Johnson, all the while wondering how come Ruby hadn't called? Why had she put that strange man up to doing her dirty work, while also wondering if he was calling to tell me my mother had died. June had encouraged me to pray, again. I'd prayed a lot as a kid, but lost the strength to continue somewhere between losing Miss Kerr that day in court and waking up in my own excrement one too may times at Guideways. Since arriving at June's I'd prayed to God to look after my mother. June had helped me see that my mother had it real hard. A mother not able to keep her kids couldn't be an easy thing, June had said.

Something had to be wrong, I thought. The only time I ever heard from anyone from my past was when one of them died: Like that time, I lived with Tom, Big Mama had called—the only time ever—and told Tom her daughter Mae Etta had passed from breast cancer. Tom told me. I thought about the five kids she'd left behind without fathers to look after them. I thought especially about her daughter, Kimberly. Death was our only connection.

"Come down to the *Marina's Edge* hotel, room 23, she should be there waiting on you."

Gwen hadn't bothered to enroll me in school. Apparently, Guideways got held up on gathering together the scraps of my school records. Also given that the local school, John F. Kennedy would soon be on Christmas break, Gwen thought it better to wait till the New Year to enroll me. And on my word that I would ask Ruby, or the man she traveled with for gas money to give her, June agreed to drive me to the hotel, to see my mother.

Room 23 had a blue door, a deep-sea-blue colored door located on the first floor near the ice dispenser. I knocked, and the door creaked open, and there in a black negligee and robe with a built-in black boa that draped twice around her shoulders stood my mother Ruby, a Pall Mall red perfectly balanced between her lips, see-through heels, a beehive hairdo and a fresh set of Lee press-on nails. Red.

"Come on now, Gina, and give your old-girl some sugar," Ruby demanded, her standard. She always had a way of talking to me as if we'd just spoke the day before, and not as if an entire decade of being gone should have anything to do with her being there right then.

"Ain't here to talk about the past, now," was her offering for any and all conversations concerning her whereabouts, and anything that might compete with the stunningness of her sudden appearance. She wouldn't illuminate her irresponsibility towards parenting.

Lebanon, her male companion, looked up when he saw June. Her auburn hair was pulled away from her face in a ponytail. Ruby didn't give her a second look, Lebanon and June exchanged looks. She decided to wait in the car, and Lebanon who'd sat up for her entrance leaned back into the dark corner, next to dark curtains. He wore dark clothing, most likely black because I do remember, at the time, thinking how he resembled a black cowboy; Stetson, boots, pants and all. Black. He stirred ice with a long handled teaspoon and it clinked up against his caramel-colored glass. A bottle of *Bacardi 151* sat in the center of the table.

"I'm here for your court date," Ruby said, to my surprise. Gwen hadn't mentioned anything about my annual custody hearing, to say nothing of my mother visiting, nor had June. Even when I'd told June about Lebanon's call regarding my mother she'd seemed as surprised as I had.

My... Mother! She was the poster child of amazement. Not only was I in the presence of the one who'd given birth to me, the one who first set eyes upon me, first held me (I imagined), smelled me, kissed me, and named me therefore making her *my* mother, but also, there I stood damn near stultified in that motel room staring at the woman who'd showed up out of nowhere, like a magic trick, her own phenomenon. I never felt that I belonged to my mother so much as I did to the astonishment of all the ways she'd lived her life.

Too afraid to ask questions, concerned that I would somehow make the dream of *my mother!* Far too real and have it all blow up in my face, I simply sat at the foot of the king-sized bed and listened to, and watched Ruby flit between having Lebanon refill her highball with spirits, and filling me in on the happenings of her two sons. How the oldest was doing well in school, and the youngest was still a little bit shy, but "He'll be just fine." Not for one moment did it seem to occur to her that I was not an old friend that needed to be "caught up" with the goings-on of her life, that I was not supposed to be hanging with her, in a motel room bordering a feeder road in some shantytown on the wrong side of Richmond. I wasn't supposed to be sitting there like some lone audience member with a front-row seat to "The Ruby Show."

Couldn't she see? I was her youngest daughter, the one she'd let slip past her watch. It was all so fantastic. A spectacle. And I was far too tongue-tied, and all twisted up inside to know what to do with all of that. I wanted, in a bad way, to ask Ruby if she'd come to take me back with her, but then I thought about Miss Kerr, I thought about everything she'd done for me, been to me. I thought about how she'd actually wanted me. Fought for me. Something in me had changed. I'd realized that although it was natural for me to call for Ruby in sadness or distress, after all she was my mother, when it came down to it, she never asked me about *me*, never really did much in the way of what I needed, wanted, told me what I wanted to hear. I would learn, later in my life, that my assessment of that moment was a concise one, and that my mother, like so many survivors of harrowing experiences didn't know how to work through her own devastation in order to show up, be there for the ones who needed them most, their children. My mother couldn't, didn't see me; she couldn't didn't see herself.

I left room 23 with the blue door one hundred dollars richer.

Ruby had sneaked it into my palm as I was leaving. "Hey, wait-a-sec, Gina-girl," she said laying her hand the same color as mine on mine and magically transferred the folded bill to me.

"They ain't feeding my baby right," she said, "You look hungry as hell," and laughed her kind of laugh, that full body thing that seemed to stop time in it's tracks and magically expunge all the loss that had defined us like vicious corrosion on a car battery.

I hadn't prayed for a one-hundred-dollar bill, but I was happy to receive it. After I paid June, I saved the rest. I guess I was trying to hold onto my mother the best way I knew how. I believed that God had answered my prayer: I was happy to see that, my Ruby, was still alive, still her wild and unusual self. Ruby made it so I only had one choice: either tolerate her or don't.

Book Three

January

1979. A placement became available in San Francisco. Gwen moved me in on a weekday when the current residents were in school. Her thinking was that it would be less disruptive, and it would give me a chance to meet the two black women she'd successfully convinced to become my "last hope."

Upon arrival at the George Walker Group Home for Girls, I met Barbra Nelson and her elderly mother, Mary Nelson. Barbra wore a beige cashmere sweater over a crisp white shirt with a popped-up collar. "I like your shoes," was the first thing I said, all of a sudden remembering Lolita's advice about Morris. Or maybe June's praying had started to soften me up a bit. "These old things," said Barbra. Those 'old 'things' just so happened to be a pair of driving moccasins by *Gucci.* She had the most perfect Afro I had ever seen, as if she'd stood in the mirror all day patting it into shape with a silk scarf. Not only could Barbra have passed as the result of a perfect collision between Native American and African American bloodlines, but also she was an identical twin to Diana Ross: pointed nose, high cheek bones and jet-black hair and large dark eyes that made her face pop. Her skin, dark toasted almond, stretch smoothly across her face, neck and hands.

"Do you have your hair done weekly? Barbra asked.

She spoke as if she were the queen of England, as if she had a mouth full of marbles. I lied, and answered "I sure do," because I wanted the new Jheri-curl perm that made black girls who needed it, look like we had good hair. I needed it. "I don't care what your life was like before your arrival here today, Regina," Miss Barbra said. Her mother nodded, Amen. "Okay." I said, unsure of what else to say. "I'm not concerned with your file, what you've done, or why, or how you did any of the things I've heard about. But here, in this house I want you to be a kid. You hear me? A kid." I heard her.

We lived in an Eichler house in Diamond Heights, and ours was the only house on the block with a bright red door and a shiny brass door knocker that made the house, from the outside, look *Hollywood* fancy. A tree grew from the middle of the open-air atrium, and we walked, every day, across thick-piled white shag carpet through two sunken living rooms, and had plenty of *Price Club* food to eat.

We sat at a dinner table, even if we just stared at one another, or the food with absolutely nothing to say, Barbra demanded we do so. We slept on nice beds with comforters and 500 percale sheets by *Marimekko*. Barbra said that just because we were black didn't mean we shouldn't aspire towards the finer things in life.

There were six of us girls and we were all shades of black. Chicana.

While the other residents at the group home chased men, dope, and empty dreams, I stayed to myself. The residents at G.W. loved to sit and share their war stories about how they ended up in foster care. I never wanted to tell anyone my business. I'd lived that madness once and wasn't about to hash it up again and again. It was hard enough hearing them talk. Didn't tell anyone about the preacher's son visiting my room every night the entire time I stayed in that house. Or the year and a half I lost in a drug-induced daze. I acted as if I were still at June's. She'd taught me a prayer I had enjoyed learning and I prayed it each night before falling to sleep:

Our Father, Who art in Heaven,
hallowed be thy name. Thy Kingdom come, thy will be done on earth as it is in Heaven. Give us this day our daily bread, and forgive us our trespasses, as we forgive those who trespass against us. And lead us not into temptation, but deliver us from evil.
For thine is the Kingdom and the glory.
Amen

Someone Has Led This Child to Believe

The butter colored folder with "Regina Louise" hand printed on the tab lay on the desk in the small office where the "house parents," slept. They were not my parents in any sense of the word and I knew that and I rarely if ever referred to them as such.

'The lady on duty, Ms. Brown, an *Ogeechee* speaking woman from South Carolina was busy doing laundry. She preferred to sit out in the atrium, dip snuff, spit it out to the tune of the dryer cycle as the clothes and sneakers tumbled and thumped their way to dry. When the drying finished, she'd sort and fold our clothes to the washer cycle. She'd switch to chewing on ice chips or rocks of powdered starch.

I knew I had time to read the entire file if I wanted. I didn't waste any of it.

The file was less thick than the one I'd read at Guideways. Most of the contents were on official pleading papers, and there were a few letters. I read the most recent one from Guideways.

Guideways Treatment Center
[redacted]
Redding California
96099
503-[redacted]

November 21st, 1978

Dear Ms. Forde:

It is with restrained relief that I write this letter to you, informing you of our unanimous decision to terminate Regina from our program. From the moment she arrived at Guideways Regina became a resident who needed far more interaction than any other resident in our care, she has exhausted our staff.

Her frequent violations of the rules; touching other residents without permission, using the telephone, swimming without permission which nearly resulted in her drowning (As you know we had to rush her to Mercy hospital by ambulance.)

I was made aware-in the middle of the night-that Regina had attempted to poison the residents and staff with the incident involving her meds, and the milk container that had to be replaced.

It is only because Regina confessed to the infraction that we, the agency, did not file charges. One strength that Regina does have is an ability to express her anger fully and move quickly back into relationship. The trouble, however, is that most people she's involved with aren't so quick to recover. Regina is the most self destructive child this agency has ever dealt with.

Regards,
[redacted], MA, LCSW

I read a short note that Gwen Forde had written to Barbra Nelson.

Barbra,

I'm writing again to see if you have an opening for my client. I believe that you and your mother are the only ones who might get it through to her that she has an identity crisis, that she is a black girl in need of guidance from her own people. I don't believe that it will be an easy thing to do, I do think, however that George Walker will be a good fit for Regina.

Between you and me, I think someone has led this child to believe she is above average intelligence when she is marginal at best. When I last asked Regina what she planned to do with her life after the age of majority she told me she's planning to attend college. I believe that Regina thinks she can climb any mountain or hurdle without preparation, this is delusional, but on second thought with her vindictive and manipulative ways this child just might succeed.

Because Regina is considered high risk the county will reimburse at the highest BHI rate.

Thank you,
████████, MSW, II

Marginal

All the girls at Guideways attended an outside school that meant I'd have to as well. Barbra was all about razing the field of opportunity for the "young ladies" in her care. So, on that first day she told me that I was closer to eighteen than I wasn't, and old enough to sign myself up for school. I was ready. I'd prayed for a chance and there it was. Barbra handed me a packet and instructed me to hand it off to the counselor they were sure to assign me to.

I left with the other residents and walked through Diamond Heights canyon to school, McAteer High.

As Barbra had said I was assigned a counselor. I wanted to be in school. I needed access to library books, to people who might be able to help me become better than I was. After what I read in that file it was clear that I was on the verge of becoming a monster. I had to fix that.

After all of the considerations were given, the proficiency tests administered, taken and scored, it was decided that with the exception of math, I was functioning, academically, at grade level: I was, officially, a twelfth grader.

I met Harry, "the hippie" within my first week at McAteer High. He was a middle-aged Shawn Cassidy, smile, long hair and all. Harry taught an advanced psychology class to students who had tested high in verbal communications. Since I was the new girl everyone was interested in learning something about me. "C'mon, tell us your name, something about yourself, and where you're transferring from," Harry asked, in rapid fire. I didn't think about what came next. I spoke through the nervousness. "My name is Regina, I'm seventeen, and I turn eighteen in May. The last placement, before the one I now live in, George Walker group home for girls, was called Guideways. I was terminated for standing up for what I believed was wrong."

After class Harry caught up to me and told me how "Bitchin'" it was that I could just share what I'd shared without blinking. He said that he imagined I hadn't had a chance to apply for colleges given what I had just said. I told him how right he was, and that I'd imagined I could go to college ever since I was twelve. I told him how I attended a basketball camp at the University of North Carolina and how that was the best thing I ever experienced. "I don't have an idea how to get to college," I said. "We'll figure something out," he said. "Do you know what marginal means?" I asked Harry. He asked why and I told him. "Oh, yeah?" he asked, his eyebrows raised to his scalp line. Well you can tell whoever told you that, I said to give you a chance to speak your mind, and you'll be sure to blow theirs." That's all I needed to hear. I smiled myself though the rest of that day.

I spent every spare minute from that point on educating myself on how to become normal, blend in to the crowd of kids who everyone expected to do something great beyond high school. The house was stocked with books, shelves stuffed to capacity. I borrowed a *Webster's Dictionary* and took it everywhere I went. Not only could I look up words again, but it was a way to keep Miss Kerr with me.

I looked up marginal in the dictionary. The meaning I got from it referenced margin as the "edge" of something. Next. I pulled out a piece of ruled paper and studied the two red lines demarcating the center from the edges. In the margin I wrote: "This is not me." And that is when it occurred to me what Gwen meant. Even though I had aspirations of becoming anything I wanted, as Miss Kerr had encouraged, from Gwen's perspective I would never make it to the center because I was destined to be trapped in the margins.

Above Average

I continued at McAteer, accepted three invitations to the same Senior Ball, and accidentally got myself voted president of the choir. The vote was unanimous. I accepted the responsibility of selecting the music we sang, the types of events we participated in, and assisted in preparing the choir to sing in school talent shows. I had finally found a place where I fit right in, no explanations, no apologies, I was just a regular girl, doing regular-girl things. I joined the baseball team, and danced with Mrs. Goldberg till my body couldn't move. I didn't think about my group home life while I was in school. I didn't think about Ruby, Tom, Gwen. Anyone. I was the happiest I'd been. I was on my own.

Eventually I had to assist the two guys I'd said "No" to in regards to the prom and I promised to find them both suitable dates. Lucky for me it was easy enough because I'd made friends with many of the choir girls, and two of them, Monique, and Angela were available and excited to go.

In order to pay for my prom gown, shoes, stockings, jewelry and get my hair done at the beauty shop I took on a paper route. As a resident, I earned five dollars a week to clean my room, complete my chores, which included cleaning my room, and maybe a bathroom or two. Sometimes we'd have to help Ms. Brown or one of the other staff members set and clear the table for dinner.

Each morning before school; before any of the other girls in the house awoke; before whichever staff was awake preparing breakfast, lunches for us to take to school, I'd hop on the bike I'd borrowed from the next door neighbor and peddle up to where Amber Drive became Duncan Street which crossed Diamond Heights Boulevard in order to pick up my bundle of papers. I'd take the time to fold, and rubberband each paper, stick them in my bib and hustle up and down those hills that made up the surrounding Eichler housing communities. I had the time of my life pitching those papers into people's yards. I always smiled when I'd hit their front door. Bullseye!

By the time I turned eighteen, and every one in my class had started all that talk about our pending graduation day and what to do regarding *Grad Nite '81*. The conversation at G.W. was all about what we were going to do after we matriculated high school? As for me, someone in the downtown school district office realized I may've had the scholastic aptitude to be a senior in high school, however, I lacked nearly three year's worth of the state required credits necessary to graduate.

"What would you like to do?" My counselor, Freidna Howell, asked. The question itself was as foreign to me as it was to actually be standing in her office, in the first place. I didn't know I had options.

After a somewhat lengthy conversation with Barbra about what it meant to turn eighteen and reach "the age of majority," in foster care, I learned that legally I was at an age where I was expected to emancipate from the system. That meant I'd have to leave the George Walker group home, even if I had no where else to go. I was outraged. But there was no one to share my confusion with. So I kept hitting the books, studying, reading.

I was grateful to finally know what that word emancipate meant for me. It's was one thing to *hear* about it, and another to understand it.

I panicked. And the feeling of that moment, the fear, the terror stayed with me well into adulthood. To have no place to go. To have no one to tell that to; that was my definition of panic.

Affected

Gwen agreed that it would be in my best interest to stay another year at G. W., that I could use the extra time to come up with a plan as to what I was going to do upon graduation. Both she and Barbra made it clear that what I was asking was "unprecedented." They were not accustomed to petitioning the courts to extend my tenure as a ward of the court. They made it clear that they were gong above and beyond to make my request a reality.

"I think I can get into a college," I said, "My psychology teacher thinks I might be able to get into Antioch University or University of California, Santa Cruz." I told Gwen how Harry felt that Santa Cruz or Antioch would be best suited for me given how they allowed students to present their exams oratorically.

"You're beginning to sound so affected, Regina" I made a note to look up that word, "affected."* While Gwen wasn't necessarily convinced that I would get into any type of college she was willing to at least work on getting me the extra time.

*Having or showing an attitude or mode of behavior that is not natural or genuinely felt.

Summertime

"You could become an opera singer, you know" said Mr. Meggars, my music teacher. "Bet you'd sound great singing *Summertime*." "What's that?" I asked Mr. Meggars, who other than Harry, and Mrs. Goldberg—the dance teacher—was one of my favorite teachers. "Repeat after me," he said using two fingers to pound A minor. It was odd sounding, that key. I was afraid of it. "I can't do that," I said. "Why, not?" Mr. Meggars asked. "I'll get laughed at." "Jesse Norman doesn't care if people laugh at her, nor does Leontyne Price. You've heard the story of Marian Anderson, right?" "Who?" "What about Pippin', or Porgy and Bess?" He had my interest. "What about Porgy and Bess? I asked, and he told me, and I shared my story with him. Again, fate had intervened on my behalf.

I decided to give it one more try. He tapped the key and I repeated after him. It was odd stretching my mouth to fit over the vowels and consonants, the high notes and the lower ones too. I agreed to meet him in the choir room during lunch period. Over and over again I sang the words behind Mr. Meggars lead until I had that song archived in my cells. I'd admitted I wouldn't practice at home. Those girls I lived with came from "East Paly-alto," and the "Sunnydale Projects," and the notorious "Pink Palace," housing. They were tough. I'd never heard of projects before. The girls thought I was a bit whitewashed because I hadn't. I tried to share what I knew about opera and the stories it told.

One girl, Keisha, flat out told me: "I ain't about to be listening to that mess." No matter. My housemates weren't about to let me blast out opera even if famous black women had worked hard to make it so they could sing it professionally, on stage, in public.

Mr. Meggars handed me the application for the California Music Educational Association Music Festival (CMEA). He had nominated me to sing in the opera category. He thought I might have a chance to be seen, be heard by a college scout, or something. Like Miss Kerr, he really showed me how he believed in me. He put in the time and researched the opportunities, and gave me all the time I needed to not just learn but also improve on what I'd learned. He continued to show me how to position my mouth when enunciating sound, how to breath in order to hold the notes, send the notes. He showed me how to make the song my own. That gave me the confidence I needed to feel capable, to test my abilities.

On the day of my solo performance I wore a red and white linen pinstriped pant suit that I'd borrowed from Miss Barbra. The more I helped myself, the more Miss Barbra came around to liking and supporting me. It seemed like whenever Miss Barbra was in front of Gwen she acted one way, and when it was just us, she'd act another way. Whenever we were in public together, and someone commented on how I looked, the way I carried myself, my cheerful nature, Miss Barbra would tell them that I was her daughter. I was uncomfortable with that and I didn't know how to say as much. Since she seemed to like me so much, I asked Miss Barbra if she'd sponsor me, like one of those foreign students who traveled to America. I told her that we could change my status with the county. I even went as far as to tell her that I felt it deep in my soul that one day I was going to be somebody. I asked her if she'd provide me with the same opportunities she provided for her own daughter. I was willing to sign a contract on the grounds that I would pay her back every penny she'd invest in me. She thought I was silly.

So, there I stood in that sound proof studio, behind layers of thick glass. Mr. Meggars was at the piano. The microphone was turned on. My hands kept time to the beat in my head. The first notes of the piano made a soft tear into the room and I leaned into the microphone and allowed the weight of the fist word *Sum...mer...time...* roll up from my belly. I let the longing and the prayerful mourn roll off my tongue as if I were that little baby I sang to, as if my "mommy and daddy," were standing by, as if I were born to sing that very song.

First prize was considered a Command Performance. I received the next category down, a Standing Ovation and I was more than good with that because in less than a year I'd moved from clawing at the walls, screaming into the slit of light in the S.H.U. box, crawling on my hands and knees, and begging like a pound dog to be set free, to receiving a standing ovation for something I learned to do, for myself.

Although she may've thought I was silly for making her that offer, Miss Barbra was there waiting for me when the recital was over. I appreciated that. In a world that appeared to be ruled by extremes of 'No's', Miss Barbra's saying 'No' to one thing yet showing up for another softened my understanding. It inspired a small sense of hope.

Diagnostic Statistical Manual Of Mental Disorders

I took a trip to the San Francisco Public Library and found my way to the "Reference" librarian and was able to peruse a copy of the *Diagnostic Statistical Manual (DSM II)*. I made it my business, to find out everything I could about some of the words Gwen used to describe me in that letter to Barbra:

Delusional; Identity Crisis; Manipulative; Vindictive.

Furtively I searched for an understanding of what had happened to me, what had folks considered was wrong with me, what could I do to be different in a way that would stick, and show the adults in my life, Gwen, Barbra, and even Lula Mae should she ever want to know anything about me; that I was capable of becoming what I wanted to become. I wanted to be the first person in Barbra's group home to graduate high school; not take the G.E.D. because I wasn't disciplined enough, or willing to do whatever it took to close the gap on my own disadvantage, but actually earn a high school diploma on my own merit and attend the college of *my* choice.

I did not find what I was looking for in that manual that day. I did, however, read about "Psychosis," given I had been diagnosed as psychotic at Guideways, and the characteristics of the mental disorder: delusional, distortion of reality, hallucinations weren't behaviors I exhibited, but were more so side affects of the medications I ingested. If anything, I would consider this: that I had an adverse reaction to my childhood, to being unwanted, rejected and or pathologized for it. There was nothing to be loyal to other than my own recklessness, truancy, and the fact that no matter how hard I wanted to belong to somebody or someone, they did't want the same. It would have been so much better to tell me the truth of the situation: neither of my parents wanted me. I knew this already, in my deepest self. I felt the ambivalence of them being in my thoughts, but not in my actual presence. It was as if my entire childhood was a see-saw where my feet touched down in both worlds simultaneously; the world of belonging and the world of belonging to ghosts. I was primed for melancholy. I was handed over to ambivalence. Stuck. I wasn't sure what to grieve. I resided in a system seemingly hell bent on marginalizing my potential to want more, do more, dream of having more by the sweat of my own hands, my own intellectual capacities, my own volition.

Most Likely To Become Mayor Of San Francisco

June 1981. "Regina Louise," announced Father John LoSchiavo, the President of the University of San Francisco. "Regina will attend the University of San Francisco this fall, and we are delighted to have her," he said. My hair coiffed in soft curls, faux alligator five-inch heels, and wearing a tan dress with delicate magenta cherry blossoms beneath my black and gold graduation gown, I walked across the stage in the USF gymnasium. Barbra's daughter also graduated that day, so she was unable to attend. I'd not heard from Gwen Forde, although I had invited her.

In my wanting to get through the group home without one incident report, I took it well when I asked Barbra if I could invite Miss Kerr and was told, *NO*. I wasn't surprised. I'd attempted many times to do the right thing, ask for what I wanted instead of doing things the way I thought best to do them. I had to think about myself, though and what was in my best interest. I believed that the time would come for me to see Miss Kerr again. I just wanted to be ready for that day. So, I didn't challenge anyone about it.

Along with Holly, Martin, Colleen and Jim, my choir buddies, we each took a turn to sing our solo parts of the song I'd suggested for our graduation." I Sing the Body Electric," from the hit film

Fame. By songs' end, the entire gym, all eight hundred plus people were on their feet. "Why come you didn't call me and tell me they voted my baby, most likely to be the damn mayor of San Francisco?" I knew that voice. I turned and there stood Ruby in a purple dress. Simple. Her hair was straightened, and styled in a shoulder-length bob. Barbra had bought my high school ring as a token of how proud of me she was. She'd given it to me earlier.

Ruby surprised me when she handed me the yearbook that I thought all of my friends had taken up a collection to buy, but somehow—and Ruby wouldn't let on how—there she was, standing there with it. Like a magic trick. A Phenomenon. Spectacular.

Later, back in her hotel room Ruby called to let me know that Barbra had tracked her down, and insisted that she bear witness to something so many doubted would ever happen including her. Barbra had paid for everything. I didn't know how to be with my mother, I felt unsettled in her presence. Instead of going to her hotel room afterwards, I went with some friends Monique, Anthony. We treated ourselves to a seafood dinner in Noe Valley. I was happy.

One week after graduation, a footlocker loaded with a bottle of wine, a wine opener, a steam iron and a faux fur coat—compliments of Barbra—and the rest of my things in yet another garbage bag, I walked out of the G.W. group home, into a Yellow Cab, and headed to a friend's house. I'd received eight offer letters to all of the schools I'd applied to through the various university's Equal Opportunity Programs (E.O.P) without which, I would not have been able to attend college. Occidental College. Chico State. California College of the Arts. Antioch. University of San Francisco. San Francisco State. City College of San Francisco.

I thanked them all for their offers. And I held onto their letters as if they were the wills of testaments of rich old uncles, and aunts. I saw those offer letters as proof of my inheritance of being smart. Enough.

REPORT AND RECOMMENDATION TO THE JUVENILE COURT
OF CONTRA COSTA COUNTY

September 8th, 1980
Date of Hearing: September 8th 1980

REGINA LOUISE--#49990-(18)-
Born: May 2, 1962, Austin Texas

Family:

Father: Tom Brock (37)	2520 Downer St. Rich, Ca.
Mother: Ruby Carmichael	Texas, exact whereabouts?
Stepmom: Nadine Hathaway	2520 Downer St. Rich, Ca.
Half-sibs: Female 6 ½	With parents
Female 4 ½	With parents

CHILD'S LEGAL RESIDENCE:
The minor's residence was established in Contra Costa County in 1976 by virtue of her father's residence. The minor's mother who has legal residence in Texas.

WHEREABOUTS OF MINOR:
The minor is in the George Walker Group Home, 218 Amber Drive, San Francisco. She was placed there January 11, 1979

COUNSEL: None.
REASON FOR HEARING: Annual review
JURISDICTIONAL RECOMMENDATION:
Continue dependency under section 300a of the W & I code.
PRIOR DEPENDENCY RECORD:
6/25/76 CCC Juv Ct Adjudged dependent child, placement ordered. The last hearing was May 12, 1978.

<u>FAMILY FUNCTIONING:</u>

Mr. Brock continues to reside in Contra Costa County with his family. He has not initiated contact with Regina or this worker during the past year. Regina initiates all contacts which are very minimal and infrequent. Regina continues to try and engage him in some kind of parent-child relationship. Mr. Brock has been unwilling to be involved in any planning for Regina and has begun to deny paternity to this worker.

Mrs. Carmichael, too has made no inquiries regarding Regina's welfare that this worker is aware of. From time to time, she calls the staff and promises to call Regina and according to the group home, it upsets Regina when mother doesn't follow through. Apparently, Mrs. Carmichael has made several promises to send money or other gifts but has not followed through. Mrs. Carmichael has been separated from Regina for many years prior to 1976. She indicated that she was very young when Regina was born and was unable, for a variety of reasons, to accept responsibility for her daughter. Mrs. Carmichael indicated that she has been a good mother to two young sons born when she was more mature and able to take on parenting responsibilities. She stated that she cannot undo the injustice that she has done to Regina but she would like to be her friend and to provide support and guidance where possible. Mrs. Carmichael talked with my supervisor, Mrs. ████████ and indicted that she would contact this writer later regarding Regina's custody but to date no further contact has been made.

THE CHILD:
Regina's problem continues to be one of having to live somewhere. For all practical purposes she has been abandoned by both parents. Regina, 18 is an attractive, articulate and an extremely narcissistic and vindictive young woman.

Regina's personal needs always seem to take precedence and if things do not work out according to her plan, she creates situations to cause total confusion and chaos. This was particularly true as she approached high school graduation. Regina was able to show signs of maturity; however, it seems obvious that graduation was as much a frightening experience as it was to anticipate.

Upon meeting Regina for the first time, one is impressed with a seemingly sophisticated, mature young woman. However, after a limited amount of contact, it becomes obvious that she is very immature and lacking in self confidence. Impulse control has improved but not to the extent that she could function independently.

Regina has natural leadership qualities but is unable to handle this positive aspect of her personality. Recently Regina was terminated form her placement for behavior problems. ████████ ██████, the director at Guideways, stated that Regina was the most difficult girl they had ever had. Regina is described as charming, bright and totally destructive to any kind of organized program.

At this point and time, the goals for Regina included graduation from high school and preparation to emancipate. Whether or not either or both of these goals can be met in the next year is questionable. She has missed a great deal of school and she has not attended public school in approximately three years. She needs to develop social skills which will help her to get through school successfully and they will also help her to cope with society in general. Regina tends to deal with people very superficially or she tunes them out completely.

The progress report dated October 2, 1978 from Guideways stated that: "at times Regina is extremely uncooperative in every aspect: disobeys house rules, defiant, rebellious, rude to the girls and staff. Conversely, Regina has the capacity of being quiet, friendly, cooperative, polite and respectful to everyone in the house. Regina attempted to poison the entire Guideways facility on November 17, 1979 which was the action that finally resulted in her permanent termination.

EVALUATION:

Regina seems to have found her niche at the George Walker Group Home. She met her match in terms of two strong willed black women (director and house parent) who were not impressed with her "cuteoy" little girl antics and have forced her to accept responsibility for her own behavior.

WORKERS PLAN:
Regina is a very needy person and has a tendency to make demands seemingly to test out whether or not support is "for real." Realistically speaking she will probably leave the program when she graduates but it is doubtful that she will be emotionally secure enough to handle her life.

I will close case upon her graduation from high school.

FREQUENCY OF VISITS:
Monthly-regular consultations with group home staff.
RECOMMENDATION:
Jurisdictional:
1. Continue as 300a

Dispositional:
2. Continue as dependent child
3. Continue 361(B).
4. Continue committed to social service placement
5. Children's Shelter or Emergency Foster Home placement or replacement.
6. Costs by Contra Costa County; parents to reimburse.
7. Social Services to authorize medical, dental remedial care.
8. Social Services authorized to temporarily return minor home.
9. Review Date: February 12, 1980

Respectfully submitted,
[redacted]
Social Casework Specialist II
Contra Costa County Social Service Department

Read and considered by:
[redacted]

Take Care Of My Girl Now

August 1981. The Yellow Taxi pulled up to the curb in front of 800 Font Boulevard. I was actually at San Francisco State University. I stepped out and stalled for a moment, I wanted to take it all in. There I was, standing in front of my dorm—Mary Ward Hall. Nobody from back home in Texas would have believed it even if they were standing right there with me all googly-eyed. No girl from any of the group homes I'd lived in would have believed it either. But there I was, standing in a dream of my own making. I was far too shocked by it all to understand the value of feeling so pleased with myself for making a plan, sticking to it.

I'd planned to arrive before the dorms were flooded by families dropping their kids off, or even after the drops had been made. I didn't want to be seen exiting a cab, I didn't want to telecast that I was alone. But from the looks of the crowds, it quickly became obvious, however, that many people had that same idea. Though it was two hours before the official registration time, girls followed behind mothers while fathers and younger siblings carried luggage, pillows, stuffed animals. I grabbed my footlocker and garbage bag and walked toward the crowds that were starting to build at the registration tables on the lawns in front of Mary Ward Hall. It was magical: I was there. I...was...there!

Because no one at G. W. had ever graduated, emancipated, or gone on to attend college, there was no one to tell me what to look forward to regarding campus life. Many of those girls either went back to their families, or plotted out ways to get pregnant so that they could be placed in unwed mother's homes. Far too many were "strongly" encouraged to join the military. There, they would be sure to get three square meals a day, clothing, shelter and given that the county funded medical benefits ceased along with the ward of the court label: the military would be an alternative to having nothing. I was tired of strangers telling me what to do. I wanted to make friends, see the world through the eyes of possibility. I wanted a chance to learn to do life my way, whatever that turned out to be. I stood there for a moment, in my dream come true, scared, a little bit sad that I was alone, but also overjoyed that I'd kept my word, didn't lose sight, and did what I said I would.

My roommate, Tracy Richman, had already picked her side of the double-closet-sized room by the time I'd checked-in, picked up my information packet, keys (the first time in my life I'd ever had a set of keys to anything), and trudged my things up the elevator, to my room.

She was pretty, petite, and Jewish, my roommate. She wore her tightly coiled hair in an asymmetrical bob (shorter on one than the other), and sported hightop Reeboks with a pair of light blue distressed *Guess* jeans with three-inch zippers on the hemline. My mouth watered. Her nails were long, oval-shaped and perfectly manicured. Barbra and her daughter would often go and have their nails and toes done, so I knew a little something about that. But those jeans were a must-have. "Oh my God, you must be my new roomie!?" Tracy stated. I was relieved to feel that she didn't seem too surprised that I was black. She, her father, and her best friend, Marnie had flown in that morning from Sherman Oaks, the pinnacle of all things "valley" and Tracy was a genuine "Valley girl," before the term made its way into popular culture.

Her father, Neil moved in and out of our tiny room dropping off suitcase after suitcase on Tracy's side of the room that quickly threatened to claim mine, and Tracy did not hesitate to boss Neil around. She told Neil where to place things, how to place them and to "Hurry. Go! Get the rest." One part of me thought her completely disrespectful—the people I came from, Ruby, Tom, The Cavanaugh's would never have stood for that. I recognized it straight away because Barbra allowed her daughter to speak to her with the same sassiness Tracy displayed.

Many times, it'd been difficult to keep my mouth shut and not tell Barbra's daughter to "take it easy, that's your mother." But that was none of my business, just like it was none of mine to say anything to Tracy. I would've made myself a liar if I didn't admit I would've consigned my soul to the devil for one night to have a taste of the power of what it felt like to belong to somebody in the kind of way where one could earn the right to mouth-off without consequences. I guessed that's what families were for; to show folks how to stand their ground, learn to ask for what they wanted, to allow children to push them around until they could learn to stand up for themselves. Family, in the best sense of the word, I imagined, was the playground for shaping who people became.

There was no time for me to feel sorry for myself about what I didn't have, although my roommate's situation provided ample opportunity: Her father and Marnie helped her decorate her side of the room, her father gave her a credit card for "any incidentals" that showed up, told her he'd see her at Thanksgiving and the holiday break. And just before Neil left he turned to me and asked: "You know of any good nail salons?" Confused, I answered "Yes," without thinking about it. Neil smiled and held his hand out and said "Gimme five." I slapped his hand, smiled awkwardly and thought that was the end of it. But it wasn't. "You take good care of my girl, now?" Neil said to me over his shoulder.

In my next life.

I wanted to be Tracy.

Cool.

All things L.A.

Loved.

I wanted a father I could boss around.

Ordinary People

I settled into school as well as could be expected, made a few friends, and like most freshmen my task was to get through the general education requirements first, before I could get to the business of deciding on a major. I took electives in human sexuality, theatre, social psychology, and ethnic studies. I signed up to be a teacher's assistant for my anthropology professor. I was fascinated by how much there was to learn about people by observing their cultural practices.

My professor thought I was unusual, "exotic" and told me he'd love for me to join he and his wife in a swinger's event. I asked around about swingers, what they did, what kind of people I could expect to be there. As soon as I learned what swingers were I squashed that invite and withdrew from the class. I wanted to try new things but not with a sixty-something elderly guy who resembled a boney Santa Claus. Even still, he gave me the first A+ and I say "gave" because I wasn't sure how I earned it given I'd dropped the class.

There was so much to learn, and none of it included switching sex partners with salacious old men. I wanted to hear what everyone had to say, I wanted to be everything all at once. I noticed that many, if not all the girls I hung out with had interesting opinions about politics, religion and knew the party for which their parents voted. I had no idea what they were talking about when it came to "Democrats" and "Republicans."

"Hey Genie," said Robyn, a new friend, a Jewish girl from Laguna Beach. I let her call me 'Genie' because I heard Miss Kerr's name in it: Jeanne. "How do your parents vote? I imagine they vote blue given that you guys are black?" "Yep," I said. "How did you know that?" I was dead serious. "Duh…" Robyn teased, as if I understood automatically.

I had no idea how any adult I'd ever come into contact with voted. I was decades behind those kid's knowing, unable to keep up when conversations veered towards class or race, and I didn't know who President Ronald Reagan was or why he got such a bad rap. And to tell the truth; I didn't care. My thinking was more in line with: I couldn't afford to care. If politics couldn't hold me, or feed me, I hadn't the time to discuss it like I was related to it, or something. My politics were to remain positive, and hopeful.

I received invitations to mother and daughter "High-Noon Teas" from various sororities both black and white, but politely refused to attend. Father-daughter dances were also out of the question. I didn't want to explain to anyone why I never spoke about family, received no phone calls, letters or birthday cards, care packages to get me through finals. This was the time in my life where I began to send those things to myself.

When I received A's or B's on my report cards I'd walk over to Stonestown Galleria and treat myself to a Baskin Robbins sundae. My favorite was a Banana Royale. I'd ask for extra nuts on the bottom, layered with hot butterscotch, bananas, and two scoops of quarter back crunch. And of course I had it topped off with whipped cream. Cherry on top. I loved eating that sundae down to the very last bite. I bought birthday cards, small gifts, and wrote letters addressed to myself, but they were signed by whichever adult I decided had written me. Sometimes I made up names like Aunt Sophie, or Grandma Louise. I'd mostly put on the show for roommates, or new friends. Once I sent myself a twenty-dollar bill from Miss Kerr, for a "job well done" when I aced a sociology quiz. I used that for two trips to have sundaes. I even enjoyed it as if she'd actually sent the gift to me. My philosophy was to imagine things the way I thought they should be, and work tirelessly to bring that thing into being.

It was halfway into the semester, a Friday night, and the main campus had cleared out by the time classes had let out. There was nothing really happening in the dorms so I asked Tracy if she'd like to go and see the movie "Ordinary People." Neither of us had heard of it, and saw no harm in watching a flick about normal white people. Anyway, it starred Mary Tyler Moore. *That Girl.* I couldn't wait to laugh.

By the time Timothy Hutton witnessed his brother slip into the ocean, slit his wrist, and admitted that he was aware that his mother hated him, I was done in. Mary Tyler Moore reminded me of Lula Mae. The heaviness of the film, the brutal disregard that Mary Tyler Moore's character showed Timothy Hutton's character was enough to make me want to slit my own wrist. I left the theater barely able to walk. Tracy and I were mute all the way back to our room. I took a shower, and it was then I broke down. I scrubbed my body and cried. No, I wailed into my soapy rag. I felt as if someone close to me had died, and maybe something had; maybe what I experienced that night was a glimpse into the weight I carried, the burden of my own undisclosed grief. There was just something not right about it all. There was nobody I could call and ask what the feeling was, why it felt as though I had suddenly lost everyone, everything I liked and loved all over again.

That is the night I made a solemn vow to become a social worker, I was going to change the system, to find a way to help kids, each one at a time if that's what it took, through difficult times. I vowed to do it one way or another.

Shortly after the movie trauma—a few days later, after I regained a bit of perspective—and armed myself with righteous indignation I marched right on over to the J. Paul Leonard library. I approached the librarian, and asked: "Can you show me where I can find a book, or a few books, on how to live in the world after emancipating from the foster care system?" The librarian studied me. "What class is this for?" she asked. I told her it wasn't for a class, but that it was for me, I needed help in understanding what it meant to have gone through the system, and if there were any books that could guide me on how to be an adult, save my money, understand why I became so sad about a movie, and how I had a real hard time shaking the feelings. I gave her a lot. She listened.

"Here," she said and scribbled a line of letters and numbers onto a slip of paper. She directed me to another woman, a volunteer, who was eager to help me find the book I definitely wasn't looking for. The title was something like "Status and Transitions of Youth in Board and Care Institutions." It was more of a highly theorized report of why, and how, kids entered institutions but not ways to manage one's life after emancipation.

That day too, I made a second vow: I swore to God that one day I'd write the book I wanted to read, a book that would be there for the young girl or boy who wanted to know how to try and make sense of the great big world they'd been literally dropped-off into like a newborn in a spin cycle; a world where they wouldn't feel a need to rely on lying in order to fit in.

I vowed to make a way where there wasn't one. After all, I'd learned in my Black Studies class that was what we as black people always did. We were known for coming back for our own: this one cared for that one and we played the act of fictive kinship forward like nobodies' business. We were the original pioneers of making a way where there wasn't one. I wanted myself, and other black children lost in foster care, to be more than just ordinary; I wanted every one of us to know what it would feel like, sound like, look like to be extraordinary.

White Mother

On another trip to the library I found a book written by Jessie Bennett Sams. It was titled; *White Mother.* It was a book about two black and orphaned twins. While Veanie tended to their paralyzed father, the other, Mengie set out to find work in order to feed her sister and father, and buy a pair of shoes for both girls to share. On her journey, Mingie found instead of shoes, a woman who showed her the first piece of kindness the child had ever seen.

Miss Rossie took the little girl into her home, bathed her, feed her, and against the violent backdrop of a time in our history that was so filled with self-hate, and racist, dogma, took the risk to become an advocate for both Mengie and Veanie. Miss Rossie helped the girls by teaching them to become resourceful. She found ways to help them other than taking them as her own daughters, yet she was the only mother figure they had.

Miss Rossie was well aware of this risks she took. She was well aware that she and her family could have been run out of town or worse, hanged for what was considered a public show of affection towards two little black girls. Nevertheless, she remained in Veanie and Mingie's life until the day she lay upon her death bed and Mingie sat by her side, finally able to hold her hand.

As a result of reading that book I was better able to understand the place from where Gwen was potentially coming from. I was heartbroken for both Veanie, Mingie, Gwen and all black people. I imagined that Miss Kerr, like Miss Rossie had given me what she could. I was thankful for what she'd been able to give to me, openly. Daringly. Courageously. Given that the publisher of that book "*White Mother*" was a man named Michael Joseph, I promised to one day name my son after him in gratitude.

Closeted Holiday

Given I'd entered college through the EOP program, everything from housing, food, medical, books and all the supplies that went along with making my college experience ripe for success was included in the financial aid package I'd been awarded. I took the fact that I'd been "awarded" all that money to mean that I'd done something great in order to receive it. So, my first couple of years I dove into my studies with a fierce commitment to do my best. The way I saw it: If the folks behind the awarding needed me to perform for them by keeping my grades at an above-average mean, I was eager to please. I needed somebody to expect something from me, push me once I tired of pushing myself. In the beginning of my time spent as a student, I rarely tired of finding ways to resource the experiences I desired to have. But there came a time when my patience, and skills to respond to my needs were tested. Severely.

I'd taken all of my finals, handed in my papers and was as ready for a break as anybody else who'd pulled all-nighters and crammed in every bit of learning my brain could take in up to the last second. I studied through fraternity-boy-funded keggers that went long into the night, until the resident assistants came and threatened to call campus security to come and shut them down. No matter what, I kept hitting those books until I was satiated, over-stuffed. Fried.

I guess I hadn't paid much attention to what it meant to have the holidays come around, or what I planned to do about them. Thanksgiving seemed to have come and gone without much notice. I couldn't, for the life in me say where I was, what I ate, with whom I ate it with. Most students stayed around campus for that first Thanksgiving, given we only had two days and a weekend off and no one really wanted to make the drive, or flight, or bus ride, home. Anyway we were preparing for finals.

Unlike Thanksgiving, though—Christmas break came out of nowhere like a two-faced friend bound and determined to confuse and with a fierce bone to pick. I watched as everyone on my floor packed their bags, made their plans, loaded the trunks of their cars up with four-to-six weeks' worth of clothes—dirty ones mixed with clean, pillows and blankets for the drive. Home. I listened as my roommate confirmed her flight, discussed the details and plans of celebrating Chanukah with her family, and heard and felt the crack in her voice as the five-months of stored up homesickness made itself known. And the first time I was asked where, and with whom, I'd be spending the break I nearly choked on my own bewilderment. "Where you going for Christmas, Regina?" My friend Daula had asked? And what I knew is that I'd arrived on campus. I worked hard to be there. That's all I was concerned with. "Oh, home, of course. Texas most likely. And you?" Another lie told. *Where? With whom? What?* I'd somehow convinced myself that the dorms would always remain open, that I wouldn't have to worry about needing a place to go, but that I would be fine in the dorms, with myself. I'd find ways to keep busy, keep myself company.

The sounds that seeped through the walls were gone, no phones rang, no televisions or radios blared. The halls were not animated with voices, or movements between dorm room and bathroom, or stairwell to the next floor. The elevators stood still. I'd promised Tracy to have fun, and that I'd think about meeting her in the valley, maybe for a long weekend sometime in January, before our break was over. I hadn't traveled—anywhere—since I'd left foster care, and I imagined a trip someplace, to meet up with someone who'd expect to see me sounded good.

After I was sure Tracy had gone, I packed up a few things in a backpack, and a small, orange Samsonite suitcase I'd purchased with my first financial aid check. Just in case one of the R.A.'s came by my room to make sure everyone had checked-out, I'd be packed, and they would see that I was just waiting to be picked up. That was the story I'd planned, the lie that momentarily staved off the panic that had reached an all-time-high. But I had a plan. I'd gone out and purchased as much Top Ramen as a grocery bag could hold, a gallon of water. I'd kept bowls, cups, and silverware from the dinning hall, and almost everyone had a single-eye hot plate, although they were forbidden, so at least I had something to cook on. Ramen had no smell, so it wouldn't alert anyone that I was there.

Later that night, I heard the elevator stop at my floor, then footsteps headed towards my room. I thought I recognized the person talking to themselves out loud but I couldn't quite hear what they were saying.

"Regina? Girl, where are you?" It was my newest friend Daula. We'd met in one of my Black Studies classes. We'd both got pissed off when in class, or professor, Dr. Laura Head began preaching about how "all you black girls perming your hair may want to consider how white you all secretly want to be." Daula and I just so happen to protest simultaneously by yelling out "Uh-uh, I don't think so." I didn't respond to her knocking at my door, calling out my name.

"I know you're in there, Regina," Daula insisted. "Come on out." I couldn't. I couldn't answer her, or face her. I just could not do it. Next thing, I heard Daula twisting the door knob, opening the door, walking in. "Regina?" she called out. I felt the sting in my eyes and tried to hold back my tears, to hold my breath, bury my body into the corner of the wall to keep from crying but I could not. I let out a sound of grief so deep, that even as I recall it, see it, and write it down in—this—moment I feel the weight of the humiliation of having that young woman open my closet door and seeing me sitting there like that with my things piled on top of me. "Girl, if you don't get out of that closet," Daula said, in a playful-yet-challenging way that allowed me a chance to recover gracefully.

Daula invited me home for the holidays. I made a vow to never forget Daula and her kindness, and to one day repay that kind of generosity to whomever needed it.

Out Here Own My Own

Freshman year gave way to my second year and by the time I became a junior I was farther away from being a disciplined student than I'd hoped for. It took a while for me to get the hang of what it meant to be an adult; pay my bills (on time), budgeting the financial aid award, making it stretch from one month to the next, an entire year. Each year brought with it the challenges of my needing a place to stay over the breaks when the dorms closed, as well as throughout the subsequent summers.

One day, I asked Miss Barbra, again, if she would sponsor me, support me in such a way that all I need do is concentrate getting through my schooling, but also if I could have a place to stay over the holiday. Miss Barbra told me, "I gave at the office." A cliché signifying that she'd already participated in giving to charity. I didn't let her get to me. Although I didn't understand, I imagined she wanted me to learn to rely on myself. I gave myself time to let the sting of what she said subside. In times like that, when adults I'd hope to trust dismissed me, I learned to go shopping or, dancing, or drinking. I got it out of my system in ways that made me feel better than their words had.

It's was as if the limitations of contact—imposed by the system—in regards to how children and youth were seen at that time leaked into them, the people meant to care for us, and perhaps it was impossible for them to see us as humans in need of attachment, touch, acceptance and most of all, love.

After that incident with Miss Barbra, I was reminded of a time when I was standing outside, in front of the George Walker group home. I believe Gwen had come to bring a potential resident to visit, one of her clients. Miss Barbra had informed Gwen that I would be graduating and moving on, and she wanted to know how she might support me. I was the first resident at Miss Barbra's who aspired to graduate high school and attend college.

Gwen had cautioned Miss Barbra to be careful of how much she catered to my needs, "After all," she said, "You don't want her to get accustomed to coming back for more." That was the thinking back then. Children in foster care were considered adults the moment they turned eighteen. Although I'd been given another year—because I was in school—that extra year hadn't prepared me for anything more than catching up to my academic disadvantage. We were products of a system that had very little data that investigated the consequences of forcing us on our own before our time.

The average American kid had a room in their parent's home until they were twenty-five back then. The average American kid had a seven-year advantage over the average foster child.

Eventually, I found my way. I discovered the career center at school and the various services they offered. I was extremely hopeful the day I came across an ad for the San Francisco Bay Girl Scout Council. They were looking for College students to work as camp counselors and I knew it was the work for me. If hired, I 'd get paid and have a place to stay during the summer, as well as save the money I made to add to my school year reserves.

I applied, and was hired. My first year I came on as camp counselor. I enjoyed it so much I returned each subsequent year until I became a counselor-in-training director. I was thirty one by the time and had a seven-year-old. I'd send Michael off to London to visit his Dad's family and I'd stay stateside. Work at camp. Save money. Camp was as close as I came to feeling like I belonged in the world. I knew that I was there for the kids, and tickled to the core that I was as wild, and crazy as many of the campers. I loved making lanyards, and God's eyes, and the group photos we took on the first day of camp reminded me of the one's I did not remember having from elementary school. Camp was like the normal childhood I'd wanted. I loved learning the songs. My favorite was "Make new friends but keep the old. One is silver and the other's gold."

I learned the values of how to treat others and modeled that for the campers. The first time I learned to make rice crispy treats I ate an entire pan of them. I learned the value of leaving things better than I found them, which was part of the Girl Scout rule. It was all about honor, the Girl Scouts were. What I appreciated most was feeling a part of something that was good, something that allowed me to not just be myself, but also offered ways for me to do things differently, in a fun learning way, with others.

Secretly. I'd always wanted to be involved in the Girl Scouts. More than anything, I wanted that little Brownie dress. There was something about that dress with those pins on it that made me feel that if I could wear it, that somehow, my whole life would change, be better. I would've given my eyeteeth to sell those cool mint cookies covered in chocolate. On my honor I was bound to try and be the best pretend girl scout there was.

Book Four

You Have No Boundaries

By the time I'd reached out to Lainey, to help me learn how to save myself, I had a son, a failed marriage to his father and a decade of trials and tribulations that had arrived in biblical proportions. I did not feel as though I were at the helm of my life steering clear of disasters, and choices, which left me somnambulistic, unable to manage. It was as though the repetitive patterns I'd learned in care of not having security or knowing how to make anything stick had taken on a life of it's own, had taken to running things. Chaos had become the Master at Arms.

Feeling lost, and desperate to know I'd mimic the actions of anybody I could; how they talked, and presented themselves. I'd heard that imitation was the best form of flattery so I'd ask people, some of whom I knew as well as strangers if it was alright that I borrow their ways of being in the world, and usually, when they didn't think I was crazy they'd say "Sure go ahead." I learned to send thank you letters by watching strangers writing in café's. I learned to hold the door open for the elderly by watching men do it in public. I even learned to greet folks with a smile even when I really didn't mean it.

Wanting to practice my new skills, I'd send cards and care packages to Ruby, and her two sons. "Kill 'em with kindness," I'd heard someplace. Ruby would receive the gifts and pictures I'd send her but would never call to say she had, or thank you. By the time I got all twisted up in paying her light bills, phone bills, and sending her birthday cards like she was my child, I had to put a stop it.

I stopped trying to reconnect with my people, and my past. My son had no grandparents, on my side, no aunts or uncles. But I wasn't willing to work like a dog to get my folks to want me. The hardest thing I ever had to do was to accept that my people did not want me.

Trauma didn't take those sorts of losses into consideration before it blew through like an atomic bomb stealing lives and leaving shadows frozen in time, tattooed into place.

Was it the sappy TV commercial of the father, with his daughter and the love he showed her by walking her through all of the rights of passages of her life; high school graduation, college graduation, down the aisle on her wedding day, that first sent me into therapy? Or was it the day a co-worker in the salon I worked at confronted me? It was my first job as a hairdresser. I hadn't much money to purchase the tools of the trade; shears, combs, brushes and a blow dryer. These things were essential. I couldn't tell anybody why I did what I did; I just did things that way at that time.

I'd take people's combs and brushes and blow dryers without asking. I might've said, "Lemme use this," and before a person could protest I'd already have it in my hands, busy at work.

A new stylist came to work at our salon. Her name was Candy.

Candy had the best tools of anyone and I really wanted to work with them. So, when she put her blow dryer in it's holder once she was done with her client, I picked it up and started using it. The first day she didn't say much. Perhaps she was intimidated; after all I was the only black woman in a salon full of white girls. And many times white girls just didn't know how to approach me. Anyway, I kept this up, taking her things and using them as I saw fit.

The day came when Candy had had it with me. She came into work, her first client sat in her chair and she went for a comb or brush—and when she couldn't find what she was looking for she screamed like a madwoman. "Where are my things?" No one said anything because they already knew. Candy found me, with a client, and right there while I used her blow dryer she said: "You are the most inconsiderate person I've ever met." I didn't understand what she meant."You have no boundaries and you think that you can just take anything from anyone anytime you want." I understood that. I was horrified. I didn't know I "had" to ask. No. That wasn't it. I didn't know how to ask. I didn't know because I didn't want to hear anyone tell me I couldn't have it. My ego was far to fragile for all of that. I'd lived with what I felt was a childhood full of hearing "No."

I couldn't believe I was that dumb. I was never in the habit of judging myself with names like stupid, or troublemaker; I didn't believe in that type of spirit bashing but that day was different. I saw how unprepared I was to be in the world with other people.

I looked up the word "boundary."* And I believe that was the final break, the one that may have sent me running into Fort Help

*Something that marks the limit of another thing.

looking for someone to help me understand what boundaries were, why I hadn't any, and where I could get them? I wanted to know what it meant to have limits.

Find My What?

Once, many years into my recovery, and during a session with Lainey, I asked her "What am I supposed do with all this healing, all this feeling 'emotionally healthy' about myself?" I was dead serious. I'd worked hard to reach back into the past, grab my demons by the neck and haul them into the light and relentlessly scrutinize what had happened to me, towards a deeper sense of understanding and meaning. I wanted to know what good it was going to do to become less dysfunctional, better able to stand up for myself, acknowledge what Lainey referred to as my "felt-self." I'd began to write a little here and there, nothing significant. I brought in a piece of my writing and read it to Lainey, a piece about Big Mama, cornbread, peach flavored snuff and Daddy Newt's tobacco pipe. They were fragments. But that was how my memories came back to me; in pieces, shards, smells. Taste.

"Find your mentors* Gina," Lainey said. *Find my what?* I felt duped. All that time and money spent whooping and hollering and remembering things I did not want to remember; experi-

*Note to self: Look up the word mentor.

encing feelings I could have done without feeling and the best advice she had for me was to go and find something I knew nothing about? "I don't even know what you're talking about," I told Lainey. "What are mentors?" I asked. Thoroughly irritated. Disappointed. Secretly, I just wanted to go home with Lainey. I knew that she lived with her partner and their two children. The youngest, she'd adopted from Nepal. She'd told me, just before she went over to bring the baby home, that I was the inspiration for the adoption. That no child should be born into the world without someone to care for him or her. "What you just read to me was powerful. There must be people, women whose writing inspires you?" Lainey asked, but I couldn't think of anyone I knew personally, in that moment.

"All you need is one person, Gina, someone who'll show you the way to your greatness. Do you know of any African American women who you might reach out too?" That was not what I wanted to hear, but I listened. Halfheartedly. I walked out of our session less enthusiastic than I'd arrived. I didn't want a mentor, I wanted Lainey. I wanted Lainey to hold me, hug me, and tell me I was meant to be alive, meant to keep going. Sometimes Lainey would just come and sit next to me, help me regulate a sudden onset of emotions.

"Where did you go?" She might've asked. "Who was there with you?"

Just asking me simple questions, sometimes, was more than enough to feel the benefits of being attached, attuned. I came to see her as someone who cared. All she did was listen, modeled boundaries.

The trouble with getting "healthy" brought with it a host of *needs* I'd never considered I needed, not to mention deserved. I needed to hear that I was doing a good job, from time to time; to be able to share with someone who'd known me as a child, or a teenager, or a young adult my dreams and let them see how far I'd come. I wanted, no *needed* someone to tell me how proud of me he or she was.

Over time, I learned from Lainey that there were other ways to be touched that didn't involve sex. I learned to ask for a hug when I needed it. Boundaries in action she would say.

Where I'd never felt particularly affectionate, after working through boundary issues, and learning the differences between my "Yes's" and my "No's," learning where I ended and world began; where the world ended and I began became crucial to my healing. So, I imagined that Lainey was putting my growth to the test, by asking me to find my mentors, to see if I could truly stand up for myself and become better able to ask for what I wanted from someone. Lord knew that not only did I not know how to ask, but also, I'd rather go without than to hear a "No." Risk being rejected. But the only way through it, if I were going to drop the victim crusade, was to speak up, let my needs be known. It was time to find people, or someone who might be able to better relate to the me I was coming into.

Shortly after that meeting with Lainey, I spent time considering how I'd find, then ask a black woman to help me. Miss Barbra was out of the question. Although she had returned to school, received her Masters in Social Work, and had opened at least four more homes—I promised I'd never ask her for anything unless she first offered. I rarely if ever saw her during those times. I learned to stop leaving myself vulnerable to rejection.

I'd heard of a book: *Who's Who in America*. A guy I'd had a very brief interest in during college had made it a big deal that he was in the student version. It would've never worked, the two of us. He needed to be worshipped. I didn't have time to worship anyone. The book he mentioned was designed to capture the photo, autobiographical highlights, and accomplishments of American icons, political figures, academics, and more. I researched the profiles of women I'd heard of, whose books I'd read, and in some cases reread:

1. Maya Angelou—Writer. Activist. Educator. Author. Mother.
2. Terry McMillian—Writer. Mother.
3. Alice Walker—Educator. Writer. Activist. Mother.

From the evidence I collected it appeared that I had something in common with each woman; I too was black and I had one child. I let me myself believe that these women were smart, they knew when to stop when it came to having children. One was enough for them and being a mother hadn't seemed to interfere with them becoming successful writers.

I wrote each woman a letter, asking her to mentor me as an emerging writer. I didn't see the harm in asking; I thought all black people would jump at the chance to help another black person. I'd soon enough learn that people were just people, no matter their skin color. They had schedules, and lives and were busy building and keeping those schedules and lives. And just because someone said "No," didn't mean it was personal, about me. It just meant: No. I began to not take rejection personally.

Each writer, in her own way, politely declined to mentor me. I was honored. I was honored that they had taken the time to tell me as much.

San Francisco
March 2, 2002

Be aware of strangers today. I'd bolted upright in my bed from a crazy dream that appeared to be so real, that for a split second I was uncertain of what, who or where I was. I clutched the front of my soaked nightshirt, my heart blasting, I searched the surroundings to get my bearings: My chest of drawers, photo of my son, Stevie and I on the nightstand, my duvet, all landmarks for place, familiarity, things to bring me back. Yet still, a wave of dread stayed with me and I wasn't certain if the homeless man who'd *just* accosted me on BART was hiding somewhere in my bedroom. I had to tell myself I wasn't on BART. I was home. Safe.

Once I'd calmed down, accepted that I'd been dreaming, I glanced over at the clock. It was 9:00 A.M. I jumped out of bed. I had a 9:30 A.M. client.

Bird bath behind me, I slammed into my dress and stepped into my heels. Coat. Handbag. I moved like a Cheetah on amphetamines down the street towards 24th and Valencia. Within five minutes a Yellow Cab paused alongside me. I scooted in and we jetted towards downtown San Francisco. If I were lucky, I'd arrive at my salon by 9:45. My clients were always generous with my being late. I tried not to take advantage.

"Good Morning, Miss Regina," said my assistant, Antonio, "Didn't you get my message?" From the elevator I glimpsed into the salon as Antonio fluttered about dusting and organizing the front desk. Assuming I had a client waiting I booked it down the hall, that way if someone were waiting they'd might appreciate the hustle. "Hey Antonio," I said searching for my first appointment of the day. "What are you doing here?" he asked. "Didn't you get my message?" "No, what message?" I asked. "Sarah from *L'Oreal* canceled, girl. She had to re-schedule for another day. The Kerastase product launch is officially delayed."

Great! I was relieved. I'd forgotten about the meeting with Sarah. I had time enough, then to catch up for my next client who should've been walking in at any minute. I picked up the printed out schedule and stared at the long, blank columns. Tony must have read the expression on my face.

"If you'd listened to my message you could've saved yourself a trip, and the embarrassment of having your dress on inside out, oh, no you didn't," he said and laughed. I loved Tony. He made a day of standing on my feet, in impractical shoes, having to cut, color, weave and or style one client after the next go by in a flash. "You could've tipped me the twenty-five dollar's—plus tip—you paid for that cab ride. He must've seen the confusion on my face. "Girl, your whole day fell apart somewhere between midnight and twilight! Even crazy Dr. Sherry, who begged you to fit her in so you could 'tighten her weave' canceled." He carried on... "All I can say is Freddie Mercury is in retrograde, and she better be gone, before somebody drops a house upon her!" Antonio said. I laughed. Naturally. "What does Mercury-in-retrograde mean, exactly?" I asked. "I dunno know, child, I just heard somebody talking about it on the bus this morning. Maybe it means we ain't supposed to be here." Tony had come and wrapped his arm around my waist. "I'll make you a deal" I said, side-stepping away from him to get a gasp of fresh air. Something inside of me was pushing me to leave as quickly as possible, and Tony reeked of a dark smokey bar. "Call and confirm my clients for Saturday, and reschedule the ones who've requested an appointment for next week. Give anyone who asks my lunch hour on whatever day they want it. I'll come in early, and stay later. After that, you can go home." "Oh, Tony, one more thing, please call my son and see if he's coming home this weekend? I'll need to know if I'm picking him up." "Alright, then Girl. I'll leave you a message on your phone. Make sure you check those messages!"

I exited the lobby of the Shreve building at 210 Post and traveled east into the wind. Earlier, I hadn't been aware of the weather. I buttoned my jacket against the cold, and headed towards the Barnes & Noble bookstore on Union Square. Something in me wanted to be more than a hairstylist. Something in me wanted to explore, to speak up; to be all that I could be for my son.

I took the escalator to the second floor where the nonfiction was kept, grabbed *A Child Called It*, purchased it and hoofed it towards the Powell Street BART station.

Smokey shadows lingered behind tall buildings, snatching light from the streets. I was swift. From sidewalk to sidewalk I moved; through traffic, pedestrians, cyclists, the hot dog cart at the corner of Post and Stockton I strode to catch a ray of sun, trying hard to keep warm.

I passed the Chanel boutique on my left and dodged a red, double-decker sightseeing bus loaded down with camera-clicking Asian tourists. Through Union Square, I jetted past Macy's, Neiman Marcus, the fat black man who wore a tangerine-orange suit and sang Sinatra and held out his matching fedora for donations. Too cold to stop. I made a hard right and soared down the steps leading underground to the Powell Street BART station.

Over the public announcement system, I heard that the approaching train was headed to Daly City. I pushed through the turnstile, took the escalator two steps at a time, and glided onto the train as the doors closed.

I took an empty seat beside a woman holding her daughter. Briefly, I watched as the mother, a dark-skinned Latina with obsidian eyes and a bright smile, swept the sleeping child's hair across her forehead with a delicate brush of her fingertips. Into the little girl's ear, she dropped bits and pieces of Spanish words, whose meanings were for the little girl, alone.

I knew, by then, the root of my jealously, the marrow of my quiet rage. Whenever I witnessed love expressed between mother and daughter or father and daughter or mother and son I wanted it, too. Not only for myself, but I also wanted to have that conectedness with my own son. But he wasn't one to give it up too easily, his love. He required much in terms of love and patience, and acceptance. He made me work for it. I did.

It was easiest to love Michael while he slept, when he was ill. It was then and usually only then, that I could touch him without being accused that my touch, no matter how tender, hurt his skin or his hair. No place on his body was safe. If I pushed the issue, try and hold him longer than he preferred the result was an all-out temper tantrum.

Hugs were out of the question. Five pediatricians all confirmed one another's suspicions: Mike was angry. The divorce made it so he had to go back and forth between his dad and I. He hated it. He needed a safe zone. I became that as well as his target. In the early years, after his dad and I divorced, I insisted that Michael visit his father on weekends. My rationale: I didn't want to be blamed, later, for withholding the relationship. Michael always resisted leaving. Too invested in trying to right the wrongs in my own childhood experience I failed to listen to him. I paid the price of not listening each time he withdraw his love. I held the space. Gladly. "He'll come back to you, later," is what my friends, clients and therapist assured. I willed myself to wait for his return.

The shrieking sound of train wheels scraping and clanging against the hard metal tracks snapped me back from my reverie. The train engineer yelled "24th and Mission". I stood and waited for the woman still carrying the girl, nearly her own size, to step out of the way.

Once on the platform, I considered heading for the escalator, but on second thought, I recalled an article I'd recently read in the *National Enquirer*. According to the article, *if a woman climbed an average of 50 stairs each day, as opposed to riding the escalator, she could stand to lose 12 pounds in under a year*. I headed for the stairs.

That's when the stranger passed me. He had the sort of face that women never forget: a broad forehead, smooth skin, hazel green eyes. He was stunning. I turned and started after him. "Hey! Hey you," I said to the man in the too-short-sleeved over coat. He slowed his stride but did not stop. He turned his head slightly and looked right through me. His gaze was unsteady. Not seeing me, he turned away. "Excuse me," I said, this time louder, waving wildly. I' must've sounded slightly agitated, several people turned to see if I was speaking to them, their faces full of quiet consternation. I walked straight towards the man. He stopped and turned towards me, kept his distance. "You talking to me?" he asked. "Yes, I am," I said and stepped closer to him. "You speak to me as if I should know you?" Up close his beige-colored skin was slightly lined. Moist. Although, there was a two-inch wide bald spot that stretched from his forehead to his nape, splitting what was left of his hair into matted Afro puffs on either side of his head;

he didn't look a day over 50 years old. He did however, look a bit like *Homey the Clown.* Small beads of perspiration crowded his temples. He shivered ever so slightly. The closer I stood to him the more I inhaled light, musky, whiffs of wet dirt cocktailed with traces of an unnamable man's cologne. "Are you saying you don't remember me?" I asked, and did a quick mental check of my hair, makeup, and the double-breasted Marc Jacobs trench coat. I felt good about myself. "Why should I remember you?" "My name is… Regina." I said in an incriminating way, meant to indict him. "My, what a fine name, Regina, but I am sorry, I don't believe we've ever met. Why should I know you?" I felt a surge of terror rush through me. "I am your daughter, Tom. My mother is Ruby."

As I stood there, waiting for that stranger to recall our connection I couldn't help but think about the Ten Commandments, the one about honoring my mother and father. I'd made it so easy for them over the years. Not wanting to run them off even farther then they were I never asked for anything, I didn't sweat them with why they hadn't tried to get to know my son, me? I'd honored them the best way I knew how and for what? There I stood, face to face with a man who didn't even recognize me. For a short moment I took that *very* personally. And as quickly as I did, I also released my need to be victimized by that moment.

It was as if my ability to understand the situation cracked open, and suddenly I realized that I'd waited my entire life to stand this man down and tell him how I really felt. The longer I stood there, in silence the better able I was to hold onto the smallest part of myself, the part that had dreamt of perforating his eyeball sockets with an icepick, the part that loathed him for never loving me into calling him, "Daddy," the feral and ravenous part of me still remembered how he'd just walked away, turned his back. Just. Like. That. I'd had visions of running into him and how I would use every profanity I'd heard to curse, and shame him all the way back to his sorry mother's womb.

I stood there. Quietly. Holding myself. My rage.

"Ain't God good! Ain't it good to see you still amongst the living?" I was shocked. I couldn't believe what that man was saying to me. It was as though his body was there, but whatever spoke from him came from another source, realm. When I last heard from Tom, Barry White had just sacked him. According to him, Barry had felt concerned that his protégé's album would catapult him—Tom—to the top of the charts. Barry felt threatened, according to Tom. Tom scoffed nonchalantly, claiming that he was writing and composing songs for his comeback. When I asked about how his wife Nadine and their three children were, he said that he'd locked Nadine in the closet where she belonged. Their son was allergic to her. Their son was asthmatic. Tom seemed more coherent then, less otherworldly. "Why did you leave me, Tom?" I didn't wait for him to answer. "Why did you let me bounce all over the place like that? Thirty different families? How come I needed to go through all that when I had you? Most of those people didn't even want to see me coming. Remember Mrs. Kerr, that white lady who wanted me, why didn't you just sign me over to her? I was locked up in an institution, Tom. You knew that. In solitary confinement! I was forced to take all kinds of drugs? Why didn't you come for me?" Tom's stare bored right through me. "You're the one who abandoned me," he finally managed to say through his apparent trance.

He had my attention and had I been a braver girl, I would've pushed him straight into an oncoming train. From that point, I didn't see a reason to go on with Tom, to try and make sense out of our past. "I've been working down at sixteenth and Mission near the donut shop," Tom said. "I'm getting the near-do-wellers ready for Jesus' return. He is on his way back; you know?" Still caught up on the bramble of him accusing me of abandoning him, I worked hard to breathe my way through it, get present. I'd tried to follow what he was saying only to *actually* realize: Tom wasn't with me.

I'd done enough therapy to know when someone had split off. I'd split off many times when things became too painful to face.

I stopped, for a moment and reconsidered how Tom looked. The duck-tapped jacket, backpack, his shoes. If I'd allowed myself to feel, in that moment, the weight of that assessment it would've been absolutely and undeniably heartbreaking. I couldn't do that; I could not go to heartbreak. I'd spent far too much time there; it was my turn to let my self out. Instinctively I knew not to cry, not with him. I took a breath, counted to ten. And without warning I wanted to reach out to Tom. I wanted to grab him, kiss him and hold him and say to him that *I am here, it's me, your daughter, Regina. Everything is gonna be alright.* I wanted to grip hold of his enormous cracked hands that used to play tennis against George Sanford Brown; those same hands had once taught me how to hold a tennis racket, once taught me how to get a live worm onto a fishing hook and cast the fishing line into the water. He'd taught me how to reel in the catch. Nonetheless, in that moment, I did not know how to reel Tom in. "There's something I want to give you before you die." The words unrehearsed fell from my mouth. For the first time, Tom looked at me and stared smack dead into my eyes, as if he understood what was coming next. "I forgive you Tom," I said, "For not showing up for yourself." I paused. "I also revoke your parental rights; you are no longer my earthly keeper. I release you. You are free to go."

We both stood there clumsily in the emptiness. And even though, in some small way, the exchange didn't feel totally clean, I was willing to live with that. Neither of us had expected that encounter. And I could see that the man I once knew as my birth father had been replaced by something else, a trauma that I'd never been that close too. I could see that our chance meeting was nothing more than an opportunity to meet Tom's ghost, to reconcile my own need to speak into the void and cleanse myself of the beliefs I carried: no matter what I'd done to make myself more successful, more stylish, more beautiful, healed, and more whole; the truth remained: my people, my father, my mother were never coming for me; not in the way I'd hoped they would. But what was possible, that day, is that my father's ghost had given me a chance to hear myself say it out loud: "I forgive you." That was for me. I took back my power that day. I turned and headed for the escalator.

"Wait!" Tom's voice pulled me back around. I waited. Listened. "I got diabetes," Tom said. "The doctor says I'm doing well. I don't take their poison—insulin. I got God. Anyway, The Doc says that I'm doing just fine." It was in that moment I saw a shining innocence, an excitement in his eyes. It was as though Tom was no more than a child; a boy standing before his fifth grade class on show and tell day. He seemed so excited, and pleased with himself. I half expected him to pull the diabetes, like a pet lizard or a bag of marbles, out of the raggedy, Duct-taped backpack and hold it up for the entire class to see. "Great! I meant to say, thank you, it's nice to finally know something about my family history." I turned to leave again. "Wa…it." That time, Tom's voice wasn't as strong. It cracked. "Don't you want my phone number?" Still seeing the young boy, I took the number he'd scribbled onto an old BART. Ticket and stuffed it in my pocket. I fell in step with a small crowd that had just disembarked a train. "Wait!" Tom yelled, again. I stopped. "*How did you know it was me, Regina?*" The incredulity of Tom's question punched me like a battering ram, in the gut. *How could I not know?* "You are my father. For Christ's sake. My father." Tom just stood there. "That's the work you get to do, Tom."

Mystified. I stepped onto the jam-packed escalator. From the corner of my eye, I managed to sneak-a-peek and see, if by some shred of a chance, Tom might be watching after me. To no surprise; he was not. He could not. As I ascended from beneath the train station, my eyes fixed on him and I continued to watch.

My father slowly picked up his backpack and with both hands clasped it to his chest. I watched him disappear on the train platform.

Once outside, I stood on the concrete pavement where 24th Street intersected Mission Street. A blanket of tulle fog crept over the Mission district skyline swallowing rooftops, church spires, street signs and life-as-usual in its wake. I was four blocks from home. I began to tremble. It felt as if I hadn't actually seen Tom, and was never going to see him again. I felt as if I'd revisited the scene of an unknown departure, one that had been lurking in the shadows, awaiting its turn to step into the light, and as a result I was spinning, triggered, stunned. Punch drunk. I literally stumbled towards home.

In the second block, the outline of a neon red Martini glass, with a green olive affixed to the rim pushed through the heavy mist.

I wasn't a big drinker, but the idea of changing states sounded like a solid alternative to the guilt-bashing that was going on inside my head. *I will not drink this away. I will not drink my way through this.* Resisting the urge provided a momentary distraction. I needed that. In some ways I felt like an unfeeling monster by not bringing Tom home with me. All of what I'd learned, turn the other cheek, present the olive branch, confront the one who had offended me had failed that time. I was simply unable to connect with him. I had to let him go.

I turned onto my street, San Jose Avenue. An overwhelming desire to blame myself for Tom not recognizing me haunted me. I wanted to punish myself. Hurt myself. That way, I wouldn't have to wait another thirty years to confront anyone in the hopes of exalting a coming back together, that way, I'd be the perpetrator deserving of being left, that way there'd be no one else to hold personally culpable. It was all me and mine alone.

If I was that same little girl, I was before—the fifteen year-old me—I imagined I would've asked a counselor for one of those pink Daisy razor's they handed out at Edgar Children's shelter. I would've slammed the razor onto the bathroom floor until the razorblade popped out. I would've cut my wrist crosswise to the vein.

Frantically, I pushed through the door of my flat, wringing my hands, wondering what to do next. Running into Tom like that, once I was out of the dynamic, had thrown me. I needed to call someone. That was my usual modus operandi. Lainey and I had created a system that should anything ever become overwhelming—in between our sessions—I could call her answering machine and leave a message. Sometimes I called when I attended other people's family events, or diner parties that triggered my loss.

Other people's happiness, and familiarity, and hugging and kissing, after an hour, would become too much for me. I never felt I had anything "common" to bring to the mix when it came to—and it always came to—where I was from, what about my family, how did I grow up? Those were the usual variables that made up the average dinner party conversations I'd participated in.

I thought to call Ruby. I somehow imagined that time and distance might've calmed her, softened her defenses, and as a result she'd be able and willing to hear me, understand how running into Tom might affect me? She'd maybe say, "Now, now…Baby." I wanted someone to explain to me what had just happened. But I'd also learned from Lainey about learning to recognize a new kind of love. We'd worked hard at identifying and cutting the strings of toxic love.

Ruby was not a good choice. Anyway, I didn't have her phone number.

I thought about which one of my friends I could call? I didn't know of anyone who knew I actually had a family, once. How could I expect anyone to understand?

I didn't know how to grieve that loss, what to call it. I didn't feel entitled to my own sadness about encountering my estranged father.

Hello...

"Hello, Lainey," I spoke into the phone, "Its Gina. I just wanted you to know I ran into my father, Tom, today. I guess I'm okay. I—uh…just wanted to tell somebody." I went back to wringing my hands wondering what to do, how to feel? I paced back and forth between the hallway and my bedroom. I was glad my son wasn't home. I'd wouldn't have wanted him to see me so out of my body, or have to explain the situation.

The less I resisted the confusion, the easier it became to befriend the emotional ambush, the chaos roiling inside of me. With acceptance came relaxation. Then, there came an instant where I felt that anything was possible if I just believed it to be.

Find a piece of paper. A voice said from within. It was just like that. Not one to be told what to do, I resisted. My mind quickly flashed between images of razor blades, and alcohol. *Find a piece of paper, now.* The voice demanded. I did a cursory check through the entryway table drawers, relieved to have tried, yet failed. I walked into the living room. A copy of the *Bay Guardian* laid on top of several Sunset magazines. I picked up the newspaper. *Find a pencil.* Back to the entryway table I went, thrashing through drawers, until I found a pencil, my chest tightening. Slowly. *Sit down.* I sat down on the edge of my rocking chair, pencil perched. Like a Ouija board planchette, my pencil began to travel around the edges of the delicate newspaper. My hand moved, recording the images that flashed across my mind.

I lost track of time, but remained acutely aware of the energy that pulsed through me; it was if I were sprinting the last leg of a race, trying to get across that finish-line, first. I traveled back in time through Texas. I saw Big Mama and Lula Mae. Lula Mae leaned from her bedroom window for me to find her babies' socks and onesies the storm winds had blown off the clothes line, or else. I looked down at what I had written. I was a mixture of scared and excited; Scarecited.

Careful not to disturb the raggedy screen door that barely kept the man-eatin' mosquitas from tearin' our asses up, I leant my body into the frame and stared up at the sky. I could tell by the way the clouds move that God's gonna start cryin' soon. I wondered who had pissed the angels off this time. The white lady from the Church of the Nazarene told me that whenever somebody committed a cruel act against one of God's children, their guardian angel would run and tell him, and he would cry for their pain—that's where raindrops come from. The white lady said that when the clouds changed quickly from fluffy white to smoky gray, well that's when the angelic messengers was runnin' 'cross the heavens. And when every breath you take holds the promise of his tears mixin' with the dirt, it was guaranteed to be a grand event. Thunder! Lightenin'! And sometimes if the crime was unforgivable, he might just throw golf balls made of ice at 'em. I know one thing: I felt sorry for whoever it was this time, but I sho' was glad it wasn't me.

Timex

"Gi...nna, come on in," Lainey said. Her smile was huge. I loved the way my insides warmed when I was around Lainey. Mostly. I followed her down the short hall, into her room. I entered while Lainey bent over and turned on the sound diffuser that sat to the right of the outside door hinges. I could always count on Lainey for consistency. Her room felt warm, safe from one week to the next. Feeling especially vulnerable, I picked up a rusty/beige colored throw, and wrapped myself into a bundle, and cuddled into the middle of her sofa.

I stared at the sand trays stacked on top of one another, and searched for figurines that were black, like me. The first meeting I'd had with Lainey I'd asked if she understood emotional distresses that came in varying shades, or if she was just for and about white people's troubles. She'd laughed. Next to the figurines were shelves lined with books, their spines vertical. I checked-off the ones that were familiar to me; the ones that I'd either already read before meeting Lainey, or ones I'd gone out and purchased over the thirteen years that I'd been a client of hers: *Seat of the Soul, The Road Less Traveled, Sacred Contracts, Home Coming: Reclaiming and Championing Your Inner Child*. I looked for new ones. I wanted to know what she knew, I wanted to participate in putting my life back together.

Lainey, giant water glass in hand, eased into the dark brown leather Lazy-Boy. The foot rest sprang up and there I sat, staring at the waffled bottoms of her "therapist clogs." They were always a dark color, burgundy or brown, and matched her overly bright outfits, which were, equally absent of style. Glad I wasn't there for a style consultation. I sat for a while, staring at the table clock. Timex. Lainey, had gray-blue eyes that never left my face during our fifty-minute sessions. If I looked at her she'd smile, sometimes I smiled too. But that day, I wasn't smiling so much as I didn't know how to start. Whenever I felt choked-up in our sessions, wordless, I'd convince myself that it was my time, after all, and I could do with it what I pleased. That's the thing about paid-for relationships: I could have the last say in how things were done. "How does it feel to be here, Gina, on a day we don't usually meet?" Lainey asked. "Fine, I guess," I said. "What brings you in today?"

"You know. I left it on your answering machine." My teeth clamped down. *Is she really going to make me work for this?* "You want to talk about the message you left?" *Duh!* I inspected my fingers. Picked at my cuticles. I opened my mouth but the words get stuck. I'd hoped to be better for the incident of running into Tom. I'd done so good on that platform, hearing him, making space, working hard to not take it personally. But somewhere between leaving him, getting home, and the writing I'd lost a bit of my courage. I couldn't find *that* adult who'd stood up to Tom. I looked over at Lainey. She forced the leg rest back into place, and scooched two or so feet towards me. "Point to where it's stuck Gina." I'd agreed to let Lainey address me by my favorite name. It was the one I liked best from childhood, the one thing I kept that was good about that time in my life. "He… didn't… know… me." I managed to say. I didn't realize it, but the grief had lodged itself in my throat. "Who didn't?" "My fa-- Tom didn't know me." "How does that make you feel, Gina?" In that moment, I didn't know how I felt; everything ran together into an unsayable tightness. "I don't *feel* anything." I said sarcastically, "How would it feel if I punched you in the face?" I asked. I wanted to scream, claw at her, punch her in the face. I wanted to tear off all of my clothes and jump out of the window. I wanted her to stop asking bonehead questions she already knew the answers to. "Plant your feet on the ground, Gina," Lainey instructed. I uncurled from the position, did as I was told. She leaned a little closer and asked me if I'd like to put my hands in a more comfortable position. I sat on them. My shoulders hunched. My feet turned in. "How old are you right now?" "Thirty-eight. Why?" (I said, further irritated: *How the fuck was this helping me? What does it matter how old I am right now?*) "How old— "I'm fifteen, okay," I said. "Fifteen." "What happened after you ran into Tom?" "I went home." "Then what did you do?" "I, uh, called your machine and left a message. "Did you do anything else?" "No, but I wanted to…I wanted to… hurt… myself." "How would you have hurt yourself, Gina?" "I wanted to push my body through a tight wall of rose bushes till all there was left were pieces of me, shredded like cheese!" I panted. "Yes, Gina", Lainey said. "Go on." She encouraged. Her eyes locked on my face. The depth of my distress began to show in the collapsing expressions that took over her face; the space between her brows pleated, her lips pursed, eyes watered. "Something told me to not hurt myself, it was like when I was in solitary confinement and I was able to get to calm, stay there and give another option a chance to show up." "Gina, the harm that you wanted to do to yourself, is the hurt you've been carrying around…for years, the hurt that was possibly done when you were preverbal." Lainey said, as tears hovered in the rims of her eyes. "I wrote it all down," I said, absentmindedly. "You wrote what down, Gina?" Lainey asked. She wiped her face with a tissue, and then placed the box on the floor between us. "What happened last Friday at the BART station?" "You mean between you and Tom?" "Yeah." "How was it, to write that?" Lainey asked. "Fine, I guess. I'm not sure of what to do with it," I said. "Gina, we have just a few minutes before we need to end."

That was the part I despised the most about therapy. Just when the going was getting good, our time was up. I didn't move. I stared into space. "Where are you now Gina?" Lainey asked. I wanted more time. Even after all the years of being together, it was still difficult to ask for what I needed. "Would you like a hug?" She asked. Not wanting to come across as a charity case I hesitated. I was afraid of how good it would feel to let her hug me. I was afraid she'd have to call someone to pry my fingers loose. I stepped into her embrace, anyway.

Next door to Lainey's office building was an alcove. On many days, after a session, and when I wasn't quite ready to fold back into my life, the world, I'd nestle into that nook to close the door on the work I'd done and ease my way back to the present. That day, Lainey was only ten minutes behind me. From where I stood, I watched as she strode across the street, confidently. I wondered where she was headed? To pick up her daughters? To meet her lover? I wondered what it would be like to come home to her, as a friend, a sister or a mother?

My Lithium Should Be Kicking In...

"Hi. I'm Regina," I said, turning the chair around so that we could both get a good look at ourselves in the mirror. By then I'd managed to let the Tom incident settle down. I was back in the saddle, doing hair which offered me the chance to stay connected to myself. "What can I do for you today?" Through the mirror I watched and listened while Marybeth, a new client, attempted to describe the hairstyle she'd seen a woman in Santé Fe wearing. Marybeth pulled a clomp of magazine pages from her heavily fringed silver and turquoise purse. "Oh, you brought pictures", I said. "Great!" "Yes indeed. I know how you creative types like to have visuals to go by," she said, "I tore 'em from an old issue of *Vogue* on the plane ride to California" "Where are you from?" I asked. "Oh, we have a second home in Santa Fe. Nothing fancy. It's little, really." Santa Fe was someplace I'd wanted to visit. I'd heard other friends, and clients speak of how "magical" and or "mystical" it was. "May I have a glass of water please?" "Absolutely. I'm so sorry for the oversight, that's usually the first thing we offer." "Oh, NO! Don't worry about it," Marybeth insisted. Antonio, the finest eavesdropper on the planet handed her a bottle of *Ty'nant* water before I could ask. "My *Lithium* should be kicking in any minute now," Marybeth said as Tony led her from the shampoo bowl to the cutting chair. "I forgot to take it this morning, with the traveling, and so forth." "Did you just say you're on *Lithium Bi carbonate?*" I hadn't met anyone since I'd left Guideways who had openly disclosed they were on meds. "I was on that as a child," I said, adrenaline scorching through me. "That's impossible," my client replied, her face suddenly wide awake with curiosity. "They don't normally put kids on drugs like that. What was going on?" "I was sixteen. I lived in a residential treatment center." I wasn't a stranger to confiding certain parts of my life to my clients. Over the years I'd become quite deft in cherry-picking the moments I'd lived that more closely related to theirs; I'd learned over time that people become leery of those whose lives felt too unconventional from their own. "They must've thought you were in a pretty bad way to put you on *Lithium*. That is no small drug to mess with. They don't usually prescribe that to teenagers," Marybeth went on. "Why were you on it?" "I'm still trying to figure that out," I answered not wanting to go all the way into it. "Well," Marybeth said, "I understand what you mean and I thank God everyday for Jane, my writing coach." "What do you mean?" I asked. Suddenly very curious. "Oh, I come to town once a month to write with a professor who works out of the extension at the university, over in Berkeley. "What do you mean by 'write with'?" I asked. "She helps me write so that I can understand what I've experienced." "Oh," I said completely intrigued. "You could name your book the Lithium Diaries," I said. I couldn't believe what I was hearing. "I'll write down her name for you if you think you're interested?" "I'd love that!" I said. That was the first and last time I ever saw Marybeth Warren.

The Arm Of An Eight-Year Old

It didn't take Jane Staw, the professor Marybeth Warren had recommended, more than a few days to respond to my phone call. I wasn't sure of my intentions in contacting Jane, but whatever it was I wanted to know more about it.

A week or so, prior to running into Tom, I'd taken Lainey's advice and began writing down some of the memories we'd recovered during our sessions. The first person who'd come to mind was Miss Kerr. I remembered her birthday, August 15th. Many times on that date I'd stop what I was doing, wonder how she was, where she was, and with whom she was living her life. Nobody every spoke the words, "Sweetheart," and "Punkin'" the way she had.

"Please send me what you've got." Jane requested. I told her I only had five pages, and under the circumstances from which they were written. She wanted whatever I had. I hung up the phone and screamed, *I did it!* Someone was interested in at least reading what "I" had to say. I sent Jane my best—and only—five pages.

Three weeks had slowly crept by when I decided to call Jane, and check-in on how the reading of my pages was going? I knew nothing about protocol and not "bugging" folks when it came to getting what I wanted. Jane was kind. She just simply didn't respond. According to her out-going message she was on a month-long "nesting" retreat with her newly adopted daughter, Daphne Opal.

I resolved to wait it out.

The more I dipped into my memories, the more I began to question what I thought had happened versus what had *actually* happened. Was I to trust the image that flashed into my mind; the pipe smells that came along with the mention of Daddy Newt's name, the taste of cold watermelon doused with salt? The clear scene when that one-time, Ruby visited my sister and I, and promised I could leave with her come morning.

I followed the arm of an eight year-old, maybe, even, a seven-year-old as it moved with a fierce determination clutching onto a Safeway bag. The arm approached the driver's side of an automobile, placed the bag onto the ground, opened the door to my mother's car, pushed the drivers seat forward and placed the bag holding what I believed to be my belongings into the back seat. I remembered what I remember thinking: I'*m gonna put my bag here so that way Ruby won't forget, and leave without me*. The power and conviction of that thought and image never left me, it haunted me up to the time I began writing. Or did it? Had I made it all up? I wasn't certain; but the emotional truth of what I began to write felt right.

"Hi, Regina, its Jane Staw. Sorry it's taken me so long to get back to you. As you may know I have a new family member, Daphne—" "Hello?" I ran from my bedroom half-naked and snatched the receiver from the cradle. "Hey listen," Jane said. "I'd love to work with you. I think you have an amazing voice. It's refreshing, actually." Honestly, I had no idea what that woman meant by "an amazing voice." "Oh-okay," I said, suddenly confused. "But you've never heard me sing." I think we were both confused because of the moment of silence that followed my confession. Jane laughed gut-hard, followed by a conciliatory "Ahh—" "No, that only means, in writerly language, that you have a way of telling your story that's memorable." I remained a bit overwhelmed but that didn't matter. Finally, I had someone willing to help me. "Can you afford sixty dollars an hour?" I could. "When do we start?" I asked. "Wednesday, next week," Jane said. "Congratulations on your new daughter!" I said. "What country did you get her from?" I imagined, like a couple of my friends she gone to either Guatemala, or China, or Russia. "Ha!" Jane said laughing. Again. "Daphne Opal is a dog. She's my new girl." In the background a dog barked. We agreed that Jane would email me a time to meet with her the following week.

Each week that Jane and I met, brought with it a host of emotional ghosts, or "grief pockets" as I called them. Memories rolled in as well, and sometimes in full scenes, and at other times in slivers or fragments that arose more out of something I touched, like the pull on a chrome beaded light chain. That recollection came back as:

I was in a room. It was dark. There were several large windows, headlights rolled across the walls, and ceiling. There was a cigarette smell, a high-pitched laugh, and a man, a door slammed. A child (I don't know how old), screamed. The child walked against traffic, headlights blinded her at eye-level…

I could not string that particular moment together with any other. Although I had felt it deep in my body that somehow I saw what that child, the one in the memory, had seen.

Each week I eagerly looked forward to what became known as: Wednesday's with Jane. Each session, which by then, trailed on the heels of my meetings with Lainey, always began with me reading the pages that I'd written in the time between us getting together, times spent widening, deepening and what Jane called *polishing* the narrative. Those times became my safe place to allow my people from Texas to visit. Their forgetting me, my denial they ever existed which was evident in how I'd never discussed them with my son or anyone else became easier. Before long I could remember happier things about my childhood: the cookouts at Big Mama's, how my sister and I pretended we were Frieda Payne and sang *Band of Gold*, how my sister told me I reminded her of the snowbird in Anne Murray's song, *Snowbird*, and she sang it to me sometimes, at night when we'd both be too hot to fall off to sleep.

Soon enough, I came to recognize that the years I'd spent honing my skills in order to fine-tune a haircut, weren't so unlike those needed to whittle down a chunk of white-hot emotion into something touchable. In the end it all came down to developing the patience to craft matter into a different kind of thing. I didn't realize how the writing was working upon me. How, the more I faced my traumas, looked at them dead-on, remained willing to befriend, and therefore transform them; the more space I created within myself. The lighter I felt. The better I slept, the happier I became. Soon enough I became aware that there was something out there, in the creation that was bigger than me, better able to discern right from wrong, bad intentions from good ones, and the sooner I realized that I was also able to see that what was out there, the bigness, the beauty, the generosity of spirit was also in there; inside of me. Lainey had mirrored for me that I was worth something, life began to mirror that worth back to me.

And it was on the tail end of that recognizing that she came in, Jeanne did. Although I'd searched for her from time to time I hadn't let anyone know. Not even Lainey. I'd gone as far as to order phone books from as many states as I could, as far away as Hawaii, close as Colorado, and yet I'd found nothing.

The first time she showed up in my writing she came in a yellow jumpsuit, or was it denim? I couldn't be certain if the jumpsuit Jeanne had worn was actually yellow, back then, in the late seventy's but that is the color that came with the memory. Her voice called out to me, "Sweetheart," the way it had so long before, and that root beer brown hair of hers in ropey whorls. I didn't share her with Jane, at first; I didn't share her with any one.

I wanted to keep her for myself. Initially Jane helped me steer the books narrative towards my being a foster child who'd bounced from home to home and how the system "failed" me. That approach felt too victim driven for my tastes. To my surprise, and according to the research I did, in 2000, there were very few memoirs, (out of the one hundred thousand plus books released each year) written for or about black women.

I wanted to contribute something that spoke to why there were more black children in foster care, than there was in the general American population. I felt we needed a different way to enter into the story. If no one was paying attention to all those children floating in society's blind spot, they probably wouldn't take much notice to a story to bring attention to that fact. That's when I began to share Jeanne with Jane. In some ways losing her had been so devastatingly disrespectful from a systematic perspective that I couldn't—as a child—fully understand the weight of her presence, or her absence. "I can't believe you've been holding out on me," Jane said. "That is your story. My God! That's your story. Of course…She was your mother, the first real mother you ever had, and you lost her. She lost you. That sounds devastating. No wonder you haven't shared her." Again, I had a reason to turn my devastation into my motivation.

If It Wasn't For Your Love

After sharing Jeanne with Jane I felt a space open up inside me. Everything felt more honest, more possible. Roomy. And at that time my music tastes were all things Natalie Merchant with or with out her 10,000 Maniacs. When I heard that song of hers, *Kind and Generous*, I knew that I wanted to one day be able to say to Jeanne what the song was about—saying thank you to someone for their kindness and generosities. I actually saw myself walking up to Jeanne. We'd be at an airport and once we saw one another we'd both run towards the other as if we were the opening of a soap opera ad. We'd fall into one anther's arms, stay there for a moment then pull away, and that's when I would tell her: "I just want to say, thank you." There was also the song by Heather Headley, "If it wasn't for your love." I learned the lyrics, the licks and the melodic rhythms which gave that song it's torch song magic. I imagined my self singing it to Jeanne as another way of saying, thank you. I added the power of these two women's music to the motivational drive that propelled me towards believing that one day I would indeed meet Jeanne again. I felt it in every part of my being. And I felt happy to know that I'd have a chance to sing her my gratitude.

Leaning On The Shoulders Of Abraham Lincoln

In December of 2000, Jane explained to me what an agent was and decided it was time for me to get one. I'd spent the last five months calling up local bookstores and offering to read my "work-in-progress." I loved saying that, "work-in-progress," the infinity of it, the idea that there would always be work to be done made me feel as if I'd have something of my own if I had my writing. I'd call up my clients and invite them to my readings at Barnes and Noble stores from Berkeley to Richmond, to Walnut Creek to Borders Books in Pleasant Hill. I read at any and all literary events I could get myself involved with. I even managed to get several local newspapers to write articles about my up and coming memoir. I believed a publisher already acquired my book and told my audiences as much. I saw it in the bookstore before it was there. I'd walk to the autobiography section and visualize my book leaning on the shoulder of Abraham Lincoln, his name came before mine.

The fact that I'd have any where from fifty to two hundred audience members willing to listen to me tell them a story that was not yet bound in a sellable manuscript was encouraging to bookstore owners, Jane, and most of all me.

Our plan was to send the first fifty pages. I learned as I went along. Jane explained that with non-fiction, which is what I had written (I did not know that), we'd only need a portion of the book and a book proposal. The idea, of course, was to send a query letter out to as many agents as we liked, hook them into asking to see the book proposal, which they'd read and *hopefully* fall in love with my story. From there, the agent would use his or her connections with editors and publishers, and the next thing we were to hope for was a book deal between me and whichever party was the most interested in publishing my book. "I think it's time for you to try and find Jeanne," Jane said. "You should know if she is still alive. She might be able to help fill-in the places where you can't remember."

Someone's Somebody

Time came around to where I needed a title. At that time, I just so happen to be reading a collection of vignettes by Gloria Naylor, *The Women of Brewster Place*. It was in that first chapter, *Mattie Michael* that I came across the phrase "Someone's—Somebody." It was the scene where the character Mattie had gone searching for her son, who'd been jailed.

I felt the plead to belong in those two words.

Unsolicited Letters Of Query

It took an entire week to write a query letter. Jane advised, that given the amount of these letters agents, editors and sometimes publishers received, it was in my best interest to carefully fashion one that would not end up in a slush pile.*

I mailed the letters on, April 28th, a few days before my thirty-ninth birthday. The next day I received a phone call from the first agent. She was planning to be in San Francisco the following day and wanted to meet-up. Unfortunately I had already made plans to get away for my birthday. I made the decision to wait till I returned from my trip.

*The place where most likely illegible, unsolicited letters of inquiry too often found themselves.

It Was Indescribable

The day I returned from my seven-day cruise I found an e-mail from an agent that Jane had recommended. I couldn't believe it. The excitement of reading the e-mails subject line: I *LOVE your voice. I am completely interested in discussing further...*" was one of the most exciting things given I had a better understanding of what was meant by my "voice."

I sat down at my desk and read it again. And again. I relaxed in my chair trying to picture what I'd say to someone interested in representing my little story about me and the little black girl I was. Without hesitation, I called Jane Anne and asked her what she thought my next move should be. She said that the interested agent, a friend of hers would probably want to meet with me in person and that perhaps I'd need to be prepared to get myself to New York City. *New York City! The Big Apple!* The little I knew about New York I witnessed through the eyes of *Sarah Jessica Parker* and her posse from the HBO series: *Sex and the City*. It was a dream coming true. Although I didn't like to fly, if it meant the difference between getting an agent or not: I'd find a way to manage a five-hour flight.

Abella's e-mail instructed me to e-mail or call. I called and we arranged to meet the following week in San Francisco. It was indescribable. Several agents were interested in my story. Other than having my son there was no better feeling in the world. I marveled at my luck

Black Prada Kitten Heels

The doorman at *Campton Place* held the door open as I stepped across the threshold to a new possibility. Located in San Francisco's Union square, I'd suggested to Abella that we meet there given that her hotel, and my salon were but a few blocks away. I appreciated the dependable service, it's atmosphere of elegant quietude. After Stevie and I opened our salon in the Shreve building; a block way, her mother Anne treated us to dinner for five nights straight at "Campton Place".

"Hey There!" Abella shouted out as she made her way to our table, "Sorry I'm a little late." "Not even," I said. She wore dark-rimmed glasses, black *Sven* clogs—the kind nurses wear, black Capri slacks and a multi-colored blouse. From the magazines I'd snooped through, the *New York* look was more like trenched coats, folded-hem jeans and black Prada kitten heels. Secretly I expected something like that. After all, she did come from the fashion capital of the world. "I'm so glad we could meet," she started off. "The timing is sort of ironic in that, I'm also in town to scout out a place to open our agency's West Coast office." "Get outta here," I said. "Serendipitous right? Abella said. "Anyway, let's talk about you, and this amazing story you've written." I wondered if I'd heard her correctly? Had she said my story was *amazing*? I knew then that I had to take what was happening—so fast—

seriously. After I met with Abella, a week later I had lunch with the big celebrity New York agent who represented famous authors from adult popular-fiction to African-American young adult novelists. She told me my story should be situated in a beauty shop given that was how *we*—meaning black folks—usually congregated. I didn't think my story was *that* book at that time. So I chose to work with Abella. I'd recently read an article about an American author—Sarah Ban Breathnach, and how thirty editors had rejected her manuscript before an editor at Warner Books acquired it. I thought that was really kind of that editor. I'd also read that I needed to imagine what I wanted for myself regarding my book. I'd grabbed the pink-section of the San Francisco Chronicle, and flipped to the *New York Times*' booklist. I cut out that section and put a line of whiteout through the number one book on the list and printed in the name of mine, instead. I'd asked Abella in one of our conversations if she thought, like J.K. Rawlings, I might get a two-book contract, and maybe even a million dollars? Abella, composed as ever advised me of what her last client received for her memoir, and that it was nowhere near a million, not to mention a two book deal. I hadn't believed her. Nothing in me wanted to, and another something in me said, *believing is seeing*. I saw it; I wrote down that I was going to get a two-book deal.

The day I left for New York City, I opened my checkbook to the ledgers page and jotted down the six-figure numbers I believed my story was worth.

I Was In A Superstar Film

"This reminds me of the *Bluest Eye*," An editor from Little—Brown said. Abella and I sat across from her. Hers was an imprint of one of the seventh largest publishing houses in the world, Time Warner Books. I'd heard of the *Bluest Eye*, had a copy of it, browsed through a few of its pages and put it down; I hadn't felt smart enough to appreciate the complexity of the narrative, what it was trying to say. Two days prior, on September 29th, I'd arrived by train at Penn Station and taken a taxi to South of Houston, (which I was instructed to pronounce—How-ston), unless I wanted to telegraph I was a tourist and risk having to pay a higher fair. I was to stay in Abella mothers' flat near the Hudson River. It was something out of a fairytale my arrival was. After debarking the train, a Red Cap grabbed my suitcase and escorted me to a set of escalators. I felt like I was in a superstar film the way I ascended from beneath that dazzling city and stepped onto the street, Pennsylvania Avenue. The closest I'd ever been to Pennsylvania Avenue was on a *Monopoly* game board, when I'd buy up the railroads first chance I got. I was thrown back that there really was such a place. Each of those few days I awoke in New York City brought with it a meeting with this person, and that one. From the moment I awoke, till the time I dropped, fully clothed, onto the bed at the end of a totally packed day, was about who wanted the book as it was, who wanted me to change the name because phonetically it confused people, and lastly who wanted me to make it about Jeanne being a lesbian so that I might ride the tailwinds of E. Lynn Harris' work. I stuck to my story, the way it was. I remained open to changing the title.

The Ancestors

On my last day in New York, Friday, I decided to ditch Abella's agenda in favor of my own. I left the house before she called and left a message with her mother regarding all the different places she'd expect me to meet her. Secretly, I didn't want to be around should those fancy editors call from their big sky-scraping offices telling me how good my book was, *but*... Also, I was exhausted telling the story of Jeanne and I. Each time I had seemed to hammer in the fact that even though I wrote about her, had become better acquainted with her occupying my thoughts, I also had to deal with the backdraft of it all. The sadness. Desire. I began wishing for her, wishing she could be there with me in that city, watching me run through stores like a crazed child trying on shoes, dresses, relying on the manners she'd taught me at fine dinning establishments.

For hours I walked my way through SoHo. For years, when I worked at *Vidal Sassoon*, all the stylists ever talked about was "SoHo," and the shopping, and the freedom of individuality that was expressed through hair, fashion and the varieties it all came in. From Canal Street to Broadway, on over to Broome, Spring and Prince Streets I perused through shops. I stopped in at the Kate's Paperie and grabbed a box of *Thank you* cards. I'd planned to fill them out on the train and mail them to all the editor's, Abella, the team at her agency, and her mother.

Given I didn't own a cellphone at that time—believing that I would burn brain cells at twice the rate if I did, I found a public payphone to call Joanne, Abella's mother. I wanted to check-in to see if anyone from my salon, or my son had called. "Where the heck are you?" Joanne asked, her voice higher pitched than I remembered. I told her I'd been shopping, having some fun. She told me that Abella had been calling every few minutes looking for me, and that I needed to give her a ring.

"OMG…" Abella said when she picked up the phone, "Where are you right now?" I told her where I was, what I'd been up to. "You did it?" She said and I was honestly unsure of what she meant. "I did what?" I asked. "Everyone we met with wants to acquire your manuscript." Abella said. I was quickly swooped up into hat old familiar feeling of being both scared and excited. Scarecit-ed. "The editor at Warner has made an offer." Abella told me the dollar amount and I had to do everything I could not to scream my face off. "Whoa?" I said. "What does this mean?" "It means we can either take the offer, ask for an auction, or we can ask for what you want and see what happens." It took only a moment for me to know which way I wanted go. "What do *you* want?" Abella asked. In some way, in that exact moment I felt that I wanted to honor my African ancestors. I didn't know who they were, but I also knew I hadn't come that far on my own. I, in that moment felt compelled to attribute a portion of my success to them. Also. I imagined black bodies on auction blocks, no choice, and no voice, sold to the highest bidder. In a much larger way, I imag-ined that my writing had come to me by way of them, the ances-tors. I could not in good conscious let my story be sold in that manner. I had a choice. I made it in such a way that befitted the situation.

I remembered walking into the editor's office at Warner Books. She was so kind. I told her my story and I saw the tears well up in her eyes. I appreciated that. Also, as I was walking out of her office

I saw a copy of that *Simple Abundance* book by Sarah Ban Breathnach. She was that agent who'd helped Sarah out when she needed it most. The editor Elyse, handed me a copy of Sarah's book. I was over-joyed! "I'd like to go with Warner," I told Abella. "Okay!" Abella said. I loved her calm demeanor. "And you accept the offer on the table?" "Nope. Let's start with asking for a two-book deal," I told Abella. "You got it. I'll keep you posted!"

It was Friday. We had to move quickly, I told Abella that if for some reason Warner changed their minds I had a second and third choice. She instructed me to go and buy myself a cell phone.

A "burner" phone in my one hand—should Abella need to contact me as I traveled across the country via Amtrak—and the treats from my SoHo trip in another, my luggage, I boarded the *Lakeshore Limited* that would take me from Penn Station to Chicago where I'd catch the *California Zephyr* in order to get home. I couldn't wait to get onto the train and into my little room, think back over those last few days, and smile myself all the way across our great big nation. Finally, it felt like I was truly living my very own version of the American dream. Secretly, I smiled as I imagined Cinderella would've been jealous of me.

Four days later. I stood in my salon staring out of the window at the San Francisco end of the Bay Bridge. On a clear day we could get a clean view through the maze of buildings that made up a good portion of Union Square, and where Market Street entered the Financial District. Earlier, I'd received a phone call from Abella. The editor at Warner had agreed to the two-book deal. When Abella asked how much I wanted, I told her the number I'd written in my checkbook the day I'd left for New York.

"Thank you for calling, Keter Salon, how may I help you?" I always answered the phone the same way. "Regina..." I recognized Abella's voice. I was terrified she'd called to tell me that big New York editor wanted me to know where I could shove my story and my ridiculous request. "It's a deal, she gave you what you asked for." I screamed first, closed my eyes and thanked God. "Thank you, Abella, for everything," I said and hung up the phone.

I Batpized Myself As My Own Mother

My manuscript delivery date had been set, and we were going to release my book June 2003. From the moment my editor, Elyse sent me the email letting me know her expectations I spent every waking moment writing, reading, re-writing and rereading the contents of my book. I continued my search for Jeanne Kerr and the more I wrote about her the more questions the adult part of me had regarding the child in me that she left behind. It was difficult to imagine that Jeanne had actually turned her back, had forgotten about me. In order to keep moving through the plot, to keep shaping and holding the gems I'd find between us I'd have to convince the adult part of me that the Jeanne that younger self had known: would've never have done that, disappeared, on her own accord.

The more I processed Jeanne in therapy the more sightings I had of her. I saw her in the shoulder of a woman who rounded a corner in a particular way. I'd walked upon the woman and before I could speak the truth would reveal itself, she wasn't Jeanne. I saw her in the switch of another dark-haired woman who sashayed down the street, the same way Jeanne had, her steps were quick-like. Certain. Sometimes I saw her pushing a baby carriage, and at other times her arm would be entwined in her lovers' as they ambled down the street love-sprung, and all over one another.

Once, upon recommendation of a client, and Stevie, I enrolled in a weekend self-improvement workshop. It offered its attendees: *A permanent shift in the quality of your life.* On day two Jeanne showed up. Her hair was blond then; layered. Shoulder length. While everyone else hurried through the doors to get into the room and find their seats, she'd glided in. Her entrance, and the way her clothes flowed like gossamer sheets immediately took me. I saw an angel.

The minute the workshop began, we were divvied-up by twos; the ones formed a single-file line through the room, and the two's stood opposite us. I was a one. The facilitator gave specific instructions. We were to grab the hand of the person on our right and left for balance and then, when we were ready, we were to stare unwaveringly into the face of the person standing directly across from us. The idea was, for each participant to create, and hold a space of loving kindness, by looking deeply into *your* person's eyes without breaking contact. As fate would have it: I stood opposite of Jeanne.

She was remarkable, that Jeanne. She gazed into my eyes and although she didn't exactly smile, the corners of her mouth softened, lifting her eyes ever so slightly into the most compassion filled face I'd ever seen. I felt the love and kindness she graciously held for me. I, however, wasn't so capable. I soon became overwhelmed by the fact that I couldn't shake my projections. I got caught in a cycle of rolling my eyes and sighing heavily to the point of not only crying, but also literally breaking down.

Jeanne continued holding the space. The more exact she was, the more difficult the task became for me. Before long, the woman who once handmade me a corduroy blue dress with a rainbow of colors that arched across the breastbone was there, reaching out to me. I'd worn that dress until I lost it somewhere between moving into foster home number eight and Guideways. Within seconds, I was completely disoriented and *beside* myself: What started out as me standing between two guys holding onto their hands, ended with me hovering between *Martin Luther King*, on my left, and *Jesus of Nazareth*, on the right. For a short time, it seemed as if I were caught between the Jeanne of my childhood years and the one that stood before me. Neither was real.

There I was, a forty-something year old woman, who'd obviously hallucinated in front of one hundred strangers. I nearly fainted from the public humiliation. At lunch I consumed whatever root vegetables, potatoes; carrots, radishes I could find, I'd learned over time various ways to not only bring myself back from a grief-pocket, but also to self soothe in such a way that I remained connected, to me. I was given an option to leave early. I accepted.

Safe in my apartment, I filled the bathtub. With a cooking thermometer I tested the water until it reached ninety-eight degrees—the same temperature of the womb when a baby was in utero. I put on Pachelbel's *Canon in D* and stepped into the tub. For a moment, I sat there, and simply listened to the sorrowful mourn of the violin chords, letting them in, letting them soften me. Then, ever so slowly, I dipped beneath the surface, balled my hands into fists and mouthed the scream I'd been holding for far too long. I imagined that I was inside my mother, tethered to her in spirit. I allowed the warmth, and the depth of her womb to absorb my rage, my shame, and my pain. I baptized myself as my own mother.

I continued to write. It was all going good, that is, until I received a sucker punch from Elyse.

"I need you to find someone to *corroborate* your story," Elyse asked. We were but a few months away from going to press. I'd turned in the manuscript on time, done my part, so I thought.

The word corroborate landed hard between us. Incriminating. It was as if I were being accused of lying, or worse. "What do you mean?" I asked. "This is America, what it *means* is that I need you to find someone to verify what you've asserted in your memoir." Only two weeks to find *that* someone—I felt somewhat optimistic—until Elyse also requested a photo to place on the cover of my book.

My automatic nervous system fully activated, I sat at my desk, and stared at the photos that stair-stepped across the walls in my writing studio, most of them of my son, a few, my partner Stevie Anne. There was the painting Stevie Anne had given to me on my fortieth birthday. A portrait of a little black girl. Blue dress. Peter Pan collar. Amber brown eyes. She looked as close as I could remember to what I might've looked like as a young girl, same age, same freckles, pigtails and all. Still, the tronie couldn't vouch for me, say that what I declared had happened had indeed *happened*, say that the life I lived was real, mine, and that I didn't make it all up.

While Elyse's deadline buzzed in the backdrop, I decided to try and locate my father Tom. Even though I remembered how he hadn't recognized me, I told myself he'd be better than having no one. I took BART to San Francisco. I got off the train at the same spot I'd seen him before. He was not there. He was not there each of the five days I returned. Waited

By then, I was booked-up four months in advance. I chopped, styled and sewed-in hair from Rebecca Walker to Sandra Bernhardt. In between my client's highlights, perms, color-touch ups and blow-dry's I wrote and scoured the Internet looking for Jeanne. Into the "search" box on each site I typed in what I knew about her. Marriage license? Nothing. Certificate of Birth of Child? Nothing. Death Certificate? Hesitantly, I punched her name into the search box and watched the ellipsis circle around searching for my Jeanne's death. Eventually that too came back with: Nothing. Maybe I had made Jeanne up, as well. But, there was the blue corduroy dress she'd hand-sewn. The way she called me "Sweetheart" or "Punkin?" The way she smelled of *Cream of Wheat* warmed Pet milk, vanilla and brown sugar.

Contra Costa County Department of Human Services

Loomed from the sender's envelope. "Return to Sender" if undeliverable, was emboldened beneath the county's address. I was relieved to be home the day it arrived. I nestled the large manila package in the crook of my elbow. It was a newborn.

I opened the envelope and removed its contents. A half-inch stack of pleading papers filled to the margins with legal jargon took up most of the envelopes contents. They were similar to the incident reports I'd broken into the file cabinets to read decades before. Unlike the original file, that envelop held half the contents I'd remembered. There were still the incident reports of the various violations I'd committed. There were the letters from one institutional director to another justifying my need to be "terminated." I looked for the psychiatric diagnosis of my being "Manic depressive-turned Bi-polar, gone Oppositional disorder. "Failure to attach."

I searched for the incidents regarding my time spent in the Security Housing Unit (the "SHU-box"), at Guideways Residential Treatment Center, boot-to-chest, back-to-floor, my face to concrete. Orderlies holding me down. I found nothing. There were no medical consent forms Gwen Forde had sworn my father signed in favor of my being treated with psychotropic drugs. The woman I'd spoken to at the county office had warned me of their vetting process. "We won't give you everything that's, in the file." My expectations were low.

Out from between one of the pages an envelope glided to the floor. It was small. I'd never seen it before. Once white—I imagined—it had been patinated by age a rusty-sort-of-gold.

May 17, 1977

Dear Linda Franz and Dr. Virginia Blacklidge,

I am sending a copy of this to both of you. Would like it to be known that I would like to be a foster parent, with the hope of one-day adopting Regina, if it is in any way in her best interest.

Have heard that it's very unlikely that foster home placements be granted to employees-so am aware of this.

The natural feeling of caring and loving is there. I will do anything possible to help her mature.

I feel Regina needs lots of attention and firmness as well as someone she can trust and communicate with. I feel that I meet these needs. She needs to know her limits explicitly and have them followed through. The need for lots of attention has been very evident during her stay at ECS. I'm sure you are aware of all the "incident reports."

I will gladly take Regina to therapy appointments and I also will be happy to participate in therapy with Regina if so desired.

I realize that Regina is an active and talented person in many ways and will require dedication and commitment to encourage the development of her potential. I love her and I think I fully realize the commitment I will be making.

Hopefully Regina will discuss with both of you the fact that her father told her this

this weekend that he's going to L.A. One of his songs made the ratings and another that he sings is being promoted. Regina said last time he went to L.A. like this he was gone for a year or more. Regina said that he was planning on sending for his wife and their daughters when he got settled. Regina says she doesn't wish to live with him anyway, but is hurt he is leaving.

I am looking for another job and hope to find one soon-this would also eliminate potential difficulties in being considered for foster parenting.

A move will also be required if there is a possibility of Regina being placed with me, as my apartment does not allow children. I have located several apartments, which do take children, for a change of residence.

I also do not know of any group home in Contra Costa Co. that does not have heavy drug traffic as well as being permissive sexually.

Regina has limited experiences in these areas and I feel it's unadvisable to expose her further to these elements. Regina is very impressionable and guidance and example are extremely important.

There are strong ties between Regina and her father, as well as between Regina and her grandmother and Regina and her mother. Hopefully Regina can someday feel better about her relationship with them.

I also realize one of the goals may be to reunite Regina with her kin. I will do all I can possible to help Regina mature. The commitment is here within me. I will look forward to hearing your professional opinion-what do you feel is best for Regina?

I am doing all that I can to get the foster care license. Regina needs to get into school, as well as get settled into her new home soon. Her wait to be placed has been almost ½ a year.

I would also like to be at Regina's institutional staffing on Tuesday to offer my input, or just sit in on the process. Will await your word on this, Linda.

Regina does not know of my desire to be her foster parent. She does not know that I will be sending a note along to both of you when she leaves for her appointment tomorrow.

Most Sincerely,
Jeanne Kathleen Kerr

Resume included to hopefully giving additional information on my background. I want to help Regina in any way possible, every way possible. Again thank you, Jeanne. *

Russian Red

With only a few days left to corroborate my story or else change all the names of the characters in the book, and no leads from the county's file, I became desperate. I asked Jules, a friend and fellow author, to help me find Jeanne. A correspondent at a well-known magazine, she had access to databases unavailable to people like me. I gave her Jeanne's full name, her birthdate, and approximate age.

J.'s return from NexisLexis brought a list of names and addresses that matched the information I'd given her regarding Jeanne. The results showed Jeanne living but a few miles from where I lived in Walnut Creek. That's where she'd lived when we were younger. I grabbed the list of addresses and drove to the first one on the list. I shook with expectation. Grief. Confusion. Rage that we'd possibly lived next door to one another and neither of us were aware of it. Rage that had she or anyone else bothered to only look in the white pages under my name she; they would've found me. I made sure to make it easy for anyone who wanted to.

I searched from the *Avila Garden Apartments*, located off Boulevard Way, to *Flora Apartment Homes*, on Flora drive: I remembered that place, it was where I'd gone when I'd run from the shelter decades before. Unbelievable. How she could have lived in the same place for so long was amazing to me. Since my time in care I'd moved as many times as I had in care.

"Yes?" a woman's voice answered at a condominium complex. There was no name on the front of the building, only an address. "Does Jeanne Kerr live here?" "What is your name?" The voice asked, something in the way she asked made me feel hopeful. I'd not heard Jeanne's voice in so long I imagined it had changed with age. "My name is Regina. I--" "She hasn't lived here in more than twelve years," the voice said. "Do you know where I might find her?" I asked. "No, I don't, sorry."

I made my way home. When I looked at the sheet J. had given me I realized that in my excitement I'd read the addresses incorrectly. Jeanne hadn't lived in the area for more than fifteen years. There was another address of an army base in Fort Campbell, Kentucky. I tried calling the numbers associated with the address no one answered at the first two. I tried calling any number on the base that I could get from the Internet.

"Hello?" The voice at the other end was hushed, similar to Jeanne's. "Anyone there?" "Yes. May I speak with Jeanne Kerr?" I crossed my fingers. "Yes, who is this?" the voice cracked. "Its Regina Louise, I think we may've met a—" "I don't believe so," the stranger interrupted, her voice turning a shade defensive. "Did you—" The line went dead.

"... ever work at the Edgar Children's shelter?" I'd wished to ask. That latest Jeanne and the other three I called joined the long list of crossed-off Jeanne's I had scribbled on a well-thumbed note-pad in pencil, pen and crayon. I wrote a letter to the last address on the list J. had given me. I purchased fine linen paper with rounded edges. In two lines I asked *that* Jeanne if she remembered me. I sealed the envelop with a kiss in Russian Red lipstick.

The deadline passed. I changed all the names of the characters in my manuscript, and ended up calling Jeanne, "Claire." Elyse approved a stock photo from Corbis.com of a young brown-skinned girl holding an umbrella; her identity obscured. My sense of erasure felt bone deep.

My book tour was slated for 10-cities: Berkeley, Portland, Seattle, Vancouver Oakland, San Francisco, Los Angeles, Claremont, Pasadena, ending in New York. Along the way I gave interviews and everyone asked about the "the woman in the book who once loved you?" "Do you know her whereabouts? Some asked. "Has she ever reached out for you?" others inquired. My answer was always *No.*

In between the questions I thought about the letter that sat at the bottom of my purse. In bright red letters it read: **Addressee Unknown**. Ever since it had been returned to me, a week after I mailed it, I carried it in my purse, a secret reminder that I was tired of looking for people who clearly weren't looking for me.

In Los Angeles I interviewed with Tavis Smiley. It was the first time on the tour I hadn't felt bombarded with questions about Jeanne. He focused more on my biological family and asked my opinion about my mother Ruby's inability to parent me. I was generous, I felt. I explained that I did not know, for certain, but my best guess what she didn't have what she needed to succeed as a person first, then as a mother. I mentioned something to the effect that Ruby didn't have her faculties about her, and that life for her had been hard. "You have it all," Tavis had said. "A thriving business, a well-adjusted son, a new book. What more could you ask for?" "I want someone to tell me that they are proud of me. I want someone who knew me when I was that foster girl no one wanted. I want someone to bear witness to what I've done with my life.

After the Tavis Smiley interview, back at The Mondrian on Sunset Boulevard, I headed straight to my room, kicked off my shoes and sat for a moment. Certain that I'd received the next day's itinerary from Kim-from-L.A. (My publicist); I rifled through my emails and came across a subject line that read: "I am so proud of you, sweetheart!" Had some one from Tavis' office transcribed my interview notes and sent them to me? I opened the message. Evidently an old co-worker, someone who worked with Jeanne during the time we were both at the shelter, read a newspaper article. Holly Eckwall.

She had a son, Jeanne did. He was twenty-six years old... She was on her way to California to bring him back to Alabama, where she and his father, her husband lived. "Please reach out to me once your tour is done. I don't want to be a bother." Speechless. Stunned. Knocked to six. How could I be certain it *was* her?

What Will I Call Her?

"Hello?" The voice at the other end of the line sounded hushed, similar to Jeanne's in timbre, her particular way of saying 'hello' softened me from the inside out. "You were my first child. Her words reverberated; "my first child." My ears were caverns. Even now, nearly thirteen years later, the commotion that moment stirred feels indescribable. "I have something I want to give you. It is your birthright," Jeanne said. *Me? I have a birthright? She has something to give me?* I was overrun with emotions. It had been nearly thirty years since we had seen one another. The only gift I imagined she had for me was a passport booklet to a trust fund. I imagined she'd been saving money for me the duration of our absence. "I want to make you my daughter," Jeanne said. *Her daughter?* There I was, twenty-seven years of no birthdays between us, no holidays, rites of passages celebrated, and no photos that stair-stepped up or down the walls of her den. We were both quiet. *What will I call her?*

New York City, 2003

W*hat should I wear to meet the woman who once wanted to be my mother?* It was 9 P.M. Eastern time. I was standing in the middle of the floor, in my well-appointed room at the Paramount Hotel in New York City; staring, trance-like into the mirror. I was unable to calm my nerves long enough to decide on which shoes to wear: the leopard peep-toe heels or a pair of last season's wedges, by Cynthia Rowley. I kicked both shoes across the room and peeled the wet silk blouse away from my skin. The sweaty cloth, similar to the paper-thin membrane that clings to the inside of an eggshell, was limp; tethered. The room, no bigger than a walk-in closet, was hot, sticky, making moving around in it a duty unto itself. New York City was the last stop on my tour. Apart from the early morning interviews and afternoon book signings at the Harlem Book Festival and the Schaumberg Center for the Arts and a CNN panel featuring Wendy Williams, Pamela Newkirk and a few other authors I'd never heard of before, I 'd spent what was left of the day flying through the best sights Manhattan had to offer: Bergdorf Goodman, Barneys, Godiva and last but not least, Henri Bendel. *Only the best will do I'd convinced myself.* After speaking with Jeanne on the phone that morning, I realized I had nothing to offer her. I needed to show my appreciation for her agreeing to meet me. I wanted to wipe the chalkboard clean of the Regina she thought she new. During one of our chats, Jeanne admitted to having a chocolate addiction. I power-walked twenty-four city blocks to get to the nearest Godiva store. I arrived just as the store was closing. I slipped a one-hundred-dollar bill between the space where the doors met in the middle and pleaded with the store manager, a six-foot-plus clean-shaven Asian man. He was beautiful. I told him how flawless his skin was, how Angelina Jolie-like his lips were, and *pretty-pretty*-pleased him until he let me in.

After scoring at *Godiva*, I added that treat to the blue pashmina scarf the sales lady had placed so carefully into the signature brown and white-stripped Bendel's box. I'd purchased her husband a golfing tee from *Bergdorf's* and hoofed my way back to the hotel.

It wasn't just that I loved shopping, or giving folks nice gifts as if they were family—which of course I did—it was about me not wanting Jeanne to have the wrong impression. It was important she didn't think of me as that severely emotionally disturbed little girl that was the cause of her not being able to adopt me. That was why, I imagined, she hadn't wanted anything to do with me. I wouldn't say as much when we met up, I hadn't planned to accuse her of anything, but I was aware that those thoughts were coming up for me.

By the time Jeanne's plane was finally predicted to land at La Guardia at 11:30 P.M. it had already been delayed three times. A tropical storm had flashed through New York, which had begun in Southern Florida, the city from which Jeanne had boarded her plane. The driver called at 10:00 o'clock and I ran through the lobby of the Paramount Hotel and scooted into the backseat of the Town car. I loved New York for that: I could get a hired car for near bouts the same price as a taxi. Over the wet streets we cruised, past the Lunt Fontaine theatre, where *Beauty and The Beast* had lines around the block, through *Times Square*, where life popped off all around us. I could hardly believe that I was *finally* on my way to meet Jeanne.

Upon arrival at La Guardia I asked the driver Pierre, a Dominican gentleman, to wait for me. It was true I wasn't clear how long Jeanne's plane would actually take, but still, I was willing to incur any additional cost because the last thing I wanted was to have her waiting in the rain for a taxi after flying through a storm.

The waiting area was small. Given that most of the people in the room looked as though they had been waiting and sitting for far too long there were several seats available and I took one that provided a clear view to the information monitor. Every half-hour or so I'd stand and get a close up of the updates, waited some more.

A few times I stood only to smooth any wrinkles from my skirt. I'd spent the last part of the afternoon trying to decide on flat shoes versus high heels, black versus pink. I'd brought three full-sized suitcases on the journey, and an empty one should I find myself shopping in SoHo. I had lots to choose from. I had imagined what it would be like to meet the woman who wanted to be my mother, for the first time. How would I want her to see me? Dress after dress, pants, shirts, and even a ball gown later I'd picked a chocolate colored midi skirt, a long-sleeved t-shirt and a pair of soft pink wedged Mary Jane's. I wanted to look approachable not too serious, or too New York like. I wanted Jeanne to feel comfortable, I wanted the little girl in me that had waited so long to feel good, safe. Beautiful.

At 11:45 I'd been waiting more than an hour and my thoughts moved from how exciting it was going to be to see Jeanne, to images of Jeanne dying in a plane crash. Visions of an aircraft plummeting, then twirling through the open sky not only crossed my mind again and again, but also I felt the rush of turbulence in my body. My heart racing, I had to nearly scold myself to *Stop it! Don't think those thoughts*. The scolding morphed into acceptance: *If that's the case, she crashes, I'll be okay—just knowing I've found her, that she remembered me enough to say she'd never stopped loving me. That was far more than I ever expected. I wanted to find Jeanne to simply say thank you, she offered to be my mother. Either way, dead or alive I am lucky.* I forced myself to have faith.

A Little after midnight Jeanne's flight landed. "Hi, sweetheart!" she called from the plane. "We just landed." I was beyond wanting her to arrive. It was great to hear her voice. "I'm waiting in the receiving area. Need any help with your bags?" Jeanne's phone cutout before she could answer. I left the waiting room and moved closer to the opening that led from the jet bridge. My mind began to somersault. I felt like a fraud.

What am I doing?
Who do I think I am?
How in the hell will I know that I am a daughter?
Really, Regina?!

I white-knuckled my handbag, straightened my back, heels together. I held onto myself like never before. I didn't want to appear too excited. I didn't want to be too much. People began to appear on the gangplank. A man, a woman, another man, two women. A woman wearing a black baseball cap with *Mercedes Benz* stitched in red block letters above the bill moved towards me. *That's not her*. She wore a sweater with colorful daffodils and peonies which swallowed the top half or her body. *No, that's definitely not her*. The woman acted as if she recognized me. *Tell me those are not lime green Capri pants with white polka dots; tell me those are not kitty cat socks.*

"Sweetheart?!" The gray-haired stranger with the wildlife-garden-inspired attire screamed. Loudly. And for a brief moment I was flushed with teen-aged mortification. It was official: I was definitely a daughter.

Jeanne placed her hands upon my face, leaned her forehead onto mine and simply held me. I remained speechless. When I finally said something it was to ask her to follow me. Once outside, and when we were safely in the backseat of the car Jeanne handed me a small album. I didn't dare look at it. I placed it in my handbag. We sat in silence all the way back to the hotel.

I'd reserved a room for Jeanne on the eighth floor of the same hotel I was in. We opened her door and there, on the table were the gifts I'd purchased earlier. We sat, and I offered her the boxes one after the other. The blue pashmina looked great with her skin tone. I hoped that she would see that I could pay my own way that I would not be a burden. "You shouldn't have, sweetheart," is what Jeanne said as we sat, her on the chair next to the table and me on her bed. "It's the very least I can do," I said. "Look at you," Jeanne said through the strain of holding back tears, "You're… all grown up."

I didn't know what to say, and even if I had, I wouldn't have known how to express the voluminous breadth of the indescribable. She too had grown up. Her ponytail was more than two feet long, and was streaked with gray and black and I was envious of the life she'd lived to earn them. Her skin, quite pale, was tighter to her face, her smile rested deeper into her chin. It was impossible to try and imagine the lives we'd both lived in the time when we were apart.

Them That's Got

There I was. There we both were, and all I could do was sit. I'd worked hard at learning to do just that. Sit. Wait. Watch for what showed up. An unintended advantage of being a foster child was the direct access we had to emptiness. In the spaces where our families should have been lay the remnants of our deepest desires. Once we could account for what we'd already lost, the next level was acceptance. Sitting. Resisting the urge to self-blame, self-mutilate. That was our inheritance.

I'd decided to pick my battles when it came to what I wanted to know from Jeanne regarding our estrangement. When it came down to it, I chose to realize that neither of us could go back and live the seconds, hours, or days that would turn into years of habits, rituals that created shared experiences; the ties which bound family together. Forever. No, that time was gone. And although I understood those things intellectually; my heart wished for something different. It wanted an accounting of all the time we'd been apart. It wanted to know how she could have lived knowing I was out there, in the world. It wanted to know if she was ever concerned with whether or not I was making it on my own.

I knew that we would need time. I would need time.

I knew that I would be able to forgive her, easily, for not being there. After all she wasn't my biological parent. I wasn't her burden back then. She was a kind human being willing to buck-up against a system, at her own expense in my best interest and for that I'd be eternally grateful.

When Jeanne stepped into the bathroom, I pulled the photo album from my handbag. I wanted time alone with the gift she'd handed me. My chest jack-hammered as I ran my fingers along the book's surface. It was made to resemble brown leather. I was afraid of what I would find inside. For a moment, I paused and attempted to relax. Breathe. When I could, I peeled the cover back, and there I found a handwritten inscription, which read:

A small token to acknowledge the heartfelt memories we share.
Love,
Mommie

Although I was afraid, I turned to the next page. There—in front of me—was the sweetest face. A young girl. I could tell, by her eyes, that she was kindhearted. Those delicate eyebrows. Her/my skin glistened a vibrant brown, and she/I smiled while hugging Tony-the-Tiger. I could barely take it. She appeared so content.

As for me, I couldn't remember if I loved him, the stuffed animal or not. *Had I asked for him?* Had I received him as a gift as many foster children had from a box of donations for Christmas or Easter, or for random reasons all of which were unremembered in that moment.

Where had I lost him?

In most of the photos that little face looked out—happily—at whoever stood behind the camera. And, in those few moments it became quickly apparent that I was incapable of making the connections, of jumping back in time to try and piece together what she had seen firsthand, what she had felt. Each turn of the page left me more thunderstruck than the one before it. *Where was I? When did this happen?* Questions upon questions arose until there came a moment when I had to admit it: I didn't know that girl, her hair, her style, her hugging—no—clutching onto that tiger.

I didn't know what lay behind those eyes that looked out at me, inviting me in. *What is she trying to tell me?* I felt a surge of panic as I landed on each photo. Her little Afro. Her smile. In each picture there she was, smiling. And my father was there too. Tom. The resemblance was uncanny; same wide forehead, broad nose. To see him sitting side-by-side like that, her body close to his was beautiful. God. He looked like he liked her in that moment. No matter what, I would always have that image archived even if I couldn't place it in time, even if I didn't know where we all were.

That photo was proof that we both had a father. Once upon a time.

Try as I might I couldn't make the leap from where I was—in a Philippe Stark luxury hotel in New York's theatre district, on a book tour—to the place *that* girl was asking me to remember her back to. Secretly, I'd grown accustomed to the book cover *me*, the girl in the tattered yellow dress that belonged to no one.

As much as I wanted to belong, I became suddenly aware that I was also afraid that I wouldn't know how to, that I/she/we might somehow mess it up… again. I became suddenly aware that I'd spent so much time searching to belong to someone outside of myself, that I'd rarely stopped to look for the girl, who in so many words, had to die in order for me to become who I was then, sitting in that luxury hotel. All the work I had done up to that point, with Lainey was about *that* moment, the one where Jeanne, like the best of mothers, could hand the caring of myself over to myself and I could accept the *gift* within the gift. When she handed me that photo album, she'd given me back the best part of myself.

And like the best of mothers, I was able to recognize—there—in the eyes of the girl who looked out at me from behind that photo, an opportunity. It would become my work to resurrect her, to take her by the hand and remind her of who she was, then, and validate the power of her choices, and listen to what she knew.

It would become my work to thank *her* for standing up for what she believed in, for holding us both up when the odds were seemingly insurmountable. It would become my work to learn to value all that she had done to grow us both up, all that she had done to hope against hope, all that she had done to exhibit courage in the face of doubt.

It would become my work to learn to value my own worth, to learn how to bless the child who'd done everything she could to get us our own.

Epilogue

Transcript

NPR Tavis Smiley
May 10th, 2006 | NPR Tavis Smiley
Interview: Regina Louise discusses growing up in foster care.

Host: TAVIS SMILEY
Time: 9:00-10:00 AM

Tavis Smiley Show recorded May 10th, 2006 -

Tavis: Regina Louise is a foster care advocate and frequent speaker at foster care conferences across the country. May is National Foster Care Month, for which Regina serves as an official spokesperson. Her own experiences in the foster care system were the basis for her 2003 memoir, "Somebody's Someone.' Regina, nice to have you on the program, again.

Regina Louise: Thank you.

Tavis: And you went through, I should say, how many foster homes?

Louise: Thirty foster homes.

Tavis: Thirty foster homes, and with all that said, no photos to be found from all those experiences.

Louise: Right.

Tavis: You're the spokesperson now for National Foster Care Month. Go figure.

Louise: You're gonna make me cry. (laughs)

Tavis: (laughs) I don't wanna make you cry.

Tavis: But isn't that an amazing story?

Louise: Yeah.

Tavis: Why 30 different homes?

Louise: One of the reasons, I believed, and it is a reason that still is an issue today, is the inability to match children with the families that reflect the child's values and beliefs. I, as the child, had no idea that each family I would go into just wouldn't work, for whatever the reasons. I had already met someone who I loved, and wanted to adopt me. So I'd given myself a head start, so I thought, to connect and let someone in.

Tavis: What was the rationale, the reason, or maybe rationale is the wrong word. The irrationality, from your perspective, for them not leaving you in the care of the woman, the mother who you wanted to be with?

Louise: At the time, I know for a fact it had to do with race. I'm Black, the woman who loved me and who wanted to adopt me was White. And at that time, it was just very, very-important for African-American children to remain in Afrcan-

American communities. And I get that, and I respect that. It's just that I as a child there was no real way for me to make that kind of an intellectual connection. To me, as a teenager, it wasn't about whether or not my foster parent was the same race. It was, do you get me? Do you see me? Are you willing to do whatever it takes to help me be the best I can be? This woman would take me to the theatre, the ballet, expose me to the real world. She was willing to do everything and anything she could to ensure that she made choices that supported my identity, culturally. And that's amazing. And I liked that.

Tavis: This woman actually has a name.

Louise: Yes. **MOMMY!** (laughs)

Tavis: And the way this studio is set up; you can't see this woman. This White woman who Regina referred to a moment ago is actually sitting off camera over there, and I wish that we could turn around. But the way the studio's set up, we can't do that. That said, I'm waving at her. Nice to have you on the set. (laughs)

She's here, but there's a great story that I did not know that I was connected to at all.

Louise: (laughs) Yes.

Tavis: Until you arrived on our set today.

Louise: Yes.

Tavis: Some time ago, we met first on, my public radio program. And as a result of that, you're back on the TV show now. Tell me what happened, though, the day that you appeared on my radio program.

Louise: Okay. The day I appeared on your radio program, you were actually my first interview. And you asked very provocative questions, and...

Tavis: I did?

Louise: Yes, you did. (laughs)

Tavis: I can't imagine that. But go ahead, yeah.

Louise: You asked about my biological mother. You asked me what I wanted and I told you I wanted someone to be proud of me. I was a little emotional when I left you. And I arrived back at my hotel room, I was sad. I turned on my computer, and there it was, her email: I am so proud of you, sweetheart. It was unbelievable. I couldn't imagine that I could say, okay, God, I'm tired. I'm done with you; I'm done with the whole thing, and when I let go, all the searching I did, the ringing of doorbells, making phone calls, the Peoplesearch, Nexis-Lexis. I let it all go, and in she came.

Tavis: So, when you were a youngster coming up through this foster care system and wanted to be adopted by this particular woman, the system, for whatever reason or reasons, as we established earlier, did not allow, would not allow that to happen.

Louise: Yes.

Tavis: But you are now officially adopted?

Louise: Yes! In the same juvenile courtroom which denied her petition nearly thirty years ago.

Tavis: Like, I don't wanna tell your age, but. (laughs) But you're no longer a child.

Louise: No. (laughs)

Tavis: But, go ahead and finish the story about how the two of you hooked up, go ahead and tell the story.

Louise: Right. Right, right, right, right. Okay. So, I get to La Guardia. And we spoke all along my book tour, and at one point, I remember her calling me and saying, I want to give you what you should have had as a child. And I thought, oh my God, a trust fund. (laughs) She has held money for me this whole time. Can you imagine the interest rate? Personal Chanel shopper. But I said, okay, great.

Tavis: Please, tell us exactly what it is she said.

Louise: She said I want to make you my daughter. What she didn't know is throughout my life, I had always written her name down as the contact on the "In case of an emergency" card.

Foster children don't usually have that. We don't have people who we can usually call. And so I put her name down, and I made a fictitious number, just so that anyone who wanted could see there was someone in that space. And all this time, when on my credit card applications, they would say mother's maiden name, I would use her name. So all along, I acted as if she was my mother.

So when she said I want to adopt you, we were just making it official, 'cause I already claimed her as my mother all along the way. When I got to New York, she arrived at La Guardia. And I had already called her Mommy. I'd never called any body Mama, Mommy, or Mom. And I'll tell my age. I was 41 years old when I first uttered the word Mommy.

She arrived at La Guardia, and handed me a photo album. And the very pictures that I didn't know existed, there they were. The very foster homes, the blue dress I write about, the Converse sneaker. And to think that I was asked to change the names in my book because there was no one to corroborate the story.

Tavis: So I have to stop you now, 'cause you were afraid of crying, but it ain't gonna be you, (laughs) it's gonna be me.

Louise: Okay. (laughs)

Tavis: In about 30 seconds, we both gonna be in tears. So we better, we gotta stop this now.

Louise: Okay. (laughs)

Tavis: See, if I was Barbra Walters, I would have made you cry, all right?

Louise: Oh, right. (laughs)

Tavis: But I'm not gonna do that to you.

Louise: Okay.

Tavis: Before we end this conversation, though, this is, as I mentioned, National Foster Care Month. What is the message for all those persons watching tonight, today, that you wanna get out in this month? We've heard your story. It's a good story. But it doesn't turn out that way for everybody.

Louise: Right. The message is, one person, one family, can change the life of a child. And I think my story just exemplifies that. And also I want people to hear and believe that love is never wasted. When you come into contact with children, some people feel that the child didn't take what they wanted to give them

They have no idea of the impact the love they've given a child has made upon that child's life. And it's never wasted. Those children, I can vouch for: we take every ounce of everything. We study you. We take everything you give. And we use what is given in ways that best makes sense to us as resources to stay alive, to thrive, to be something better than what we came from. Caregivers may never know the impressions they make, because many times they don't see the children after the children leave their homes.

So the message is, one person, one family, can change a lifetime.

Tavis: If I ask your mother to come on stage, and she agreed to do so, would that embarrass you?

Louise: (laughs) No, no, no.

Tavis: I'm gonna have her come sit right on the arm of this chair.

Louise: Okay. (laughs)

Tavis: Before I say goodnight.

Louise: Come on, Mom. Oh, Tavis, you're gonna make me weep. (laughs)

Tavis: There you go. That's all right. You sit right there. Nice to meet you.

Jeannie Kerr: It's a pleasure to be here.

Tavis: I'm glad to have you on the program.

Louise: Oh, wow.

Tavis: You thought I was making this up. If you thought I was, I'm not. There she is, and there they are.

Louise: Thank you.

Tavis: May is National Foster Care Month. You cannot, I suspect, be unmoved by this conversation with Regina Louise. I can assure you, you will not be unmoved by the reading of her book. It's called "Somebody's Someone, A Memoir by Regina Louise.' Nice to have you both here.

Louise: Oh, thank you. Nice to be on your show.

Tavis: That's our show for tonight. Catch me on the weekends on PRI, Public Radio International, check your local listings. See you back here next time on PBS. Until then, good night from L.A., thanks for watching. And as always, keep the faith.

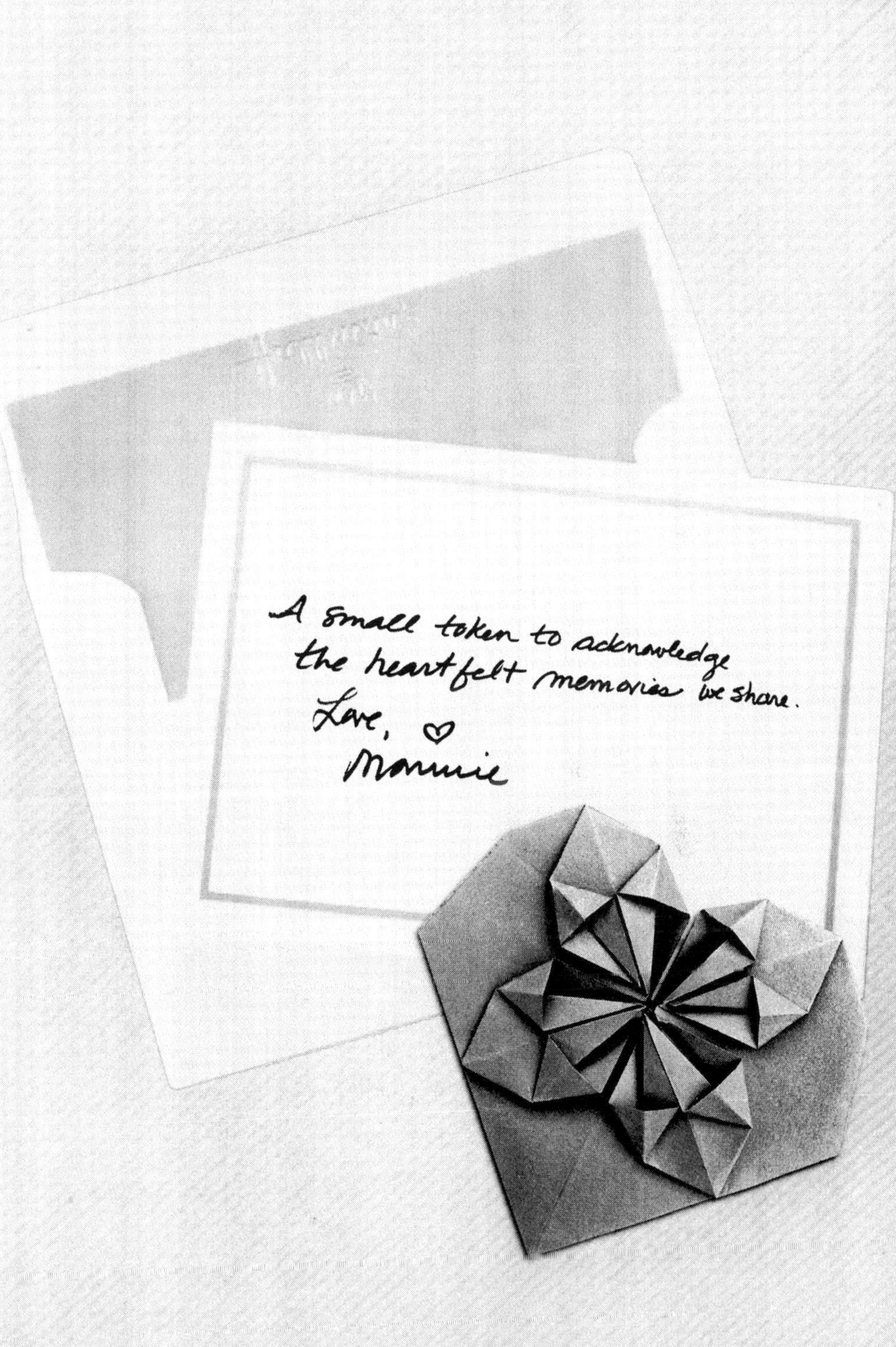
A small token to acknowledge
the heartfelt memories we share.
Love,
Mommie

Regina holding onto Tony the Tiger.

Top, Regina and Jeanne.
Bottom, Regina.

Top, Joanie, Elizabeth, Judith, Regina and Jeanne.
Bottom, Judith, Regina and Jeanne.

Top, Regina and Jeanne.
Bottom, Judith and Regina.

Top, The Kerr Family and Regina.
Bottom, Regina and Tom Brock (father).

Regina.

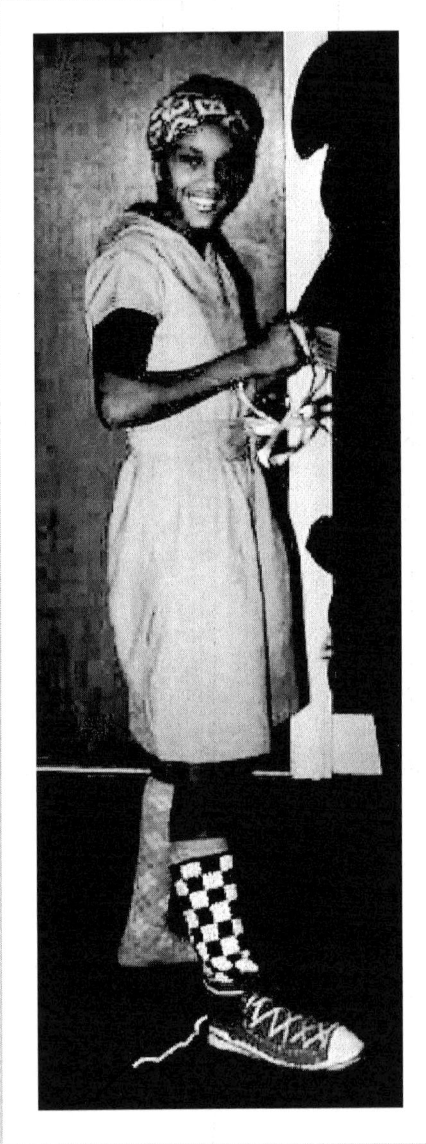

Regina.

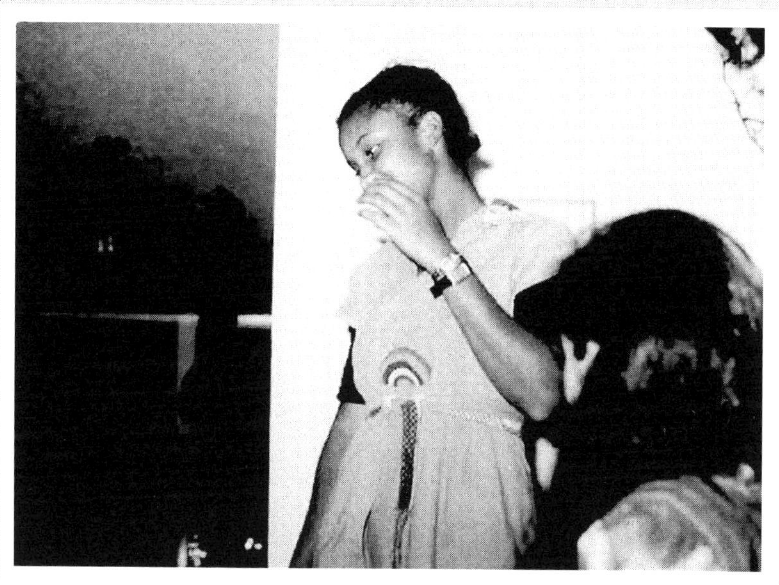

Top, Regina.
Bottom, Elizabeth, John, Regina.

Top, Regina and Mommy.
Bottom, Adoption day 2003. Regina and Jeanne's family.

The recipient of numerous awards, Regina Louise was most recently awarded the Human Services Award for reducing the number of minority children in foster care, and the Los Angeles County Board of Supervisors honored Regina for her service in helping Los Angeles County foster youth.

By the time she was 16, Ms. Louise lived in—and failed to adjust to—far too many foster homes, group homes and psychiatric facilities. The many valuable years of formal education that Ms. Louise missed didn't prevent her from pursuing her belief that she "would be somebody" and in less than three short years, Ms. Louise has addressed and educated people across the nation about the present state, and most probable futures, of youth lost in foster care adrift. From the Salish Nation Indian tribes of Northern Washington, to the depths of "Suitcase City" in Southern Florida, crowds have heard and felt the power of her message: LOVE IS NEVER WASTED.

Author of the memoir *Somebody's Someone*, Regina's story has been featured on *The BBC World Service*, *Narrative.ly Literary Magazine* and the *Epoch Times* as well as NPR's *All Things Considered*, The CBS *Early Show*, PBS's T*avis Smiley Show* and *NBC11*. Ms. Louise's story has received nationwide attention in newspapers and magazines including *The San Francisco Chronicle*, *Shanghai Times*, *Los Angeles Times*, *Hallmark Magazine*, *Philadelphia Tribune* and *The Chicago Tribune*.

Somebody's Someone has also been adapted into a one-woman-show and was the subject of an Emmy-nominated PBS documentary. The NAACP nominated Ms. Louise's one-woman show for two Theatre Awards.

Currently, Ms. Louise is a Child Welfare Executive Coach, a Key Note Speaker and Trainer.

Her next project is a young adult series. Stay tuned!